Colour and Create
Geometric Shapes & Patterns
Volume 3

50 Designs to help release
your creative side

Connect with us online to
- Share your colourings with other colouring enthusiasts
- Get free downloads of some of our designs
- Find out about our up-and-coming books
- Get discounts and enter competitions

Our Facebook Page:
www.colourandcreate.com/facebook

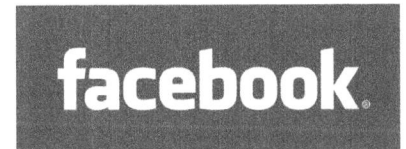

Our Facebook group:
www.colourandcreate.com/facebookgroup

On Twitter:
www.colourandcreate.com/twitter

On Pinterest:
www.colourandcreate.com/pinterest

Colour Test Page

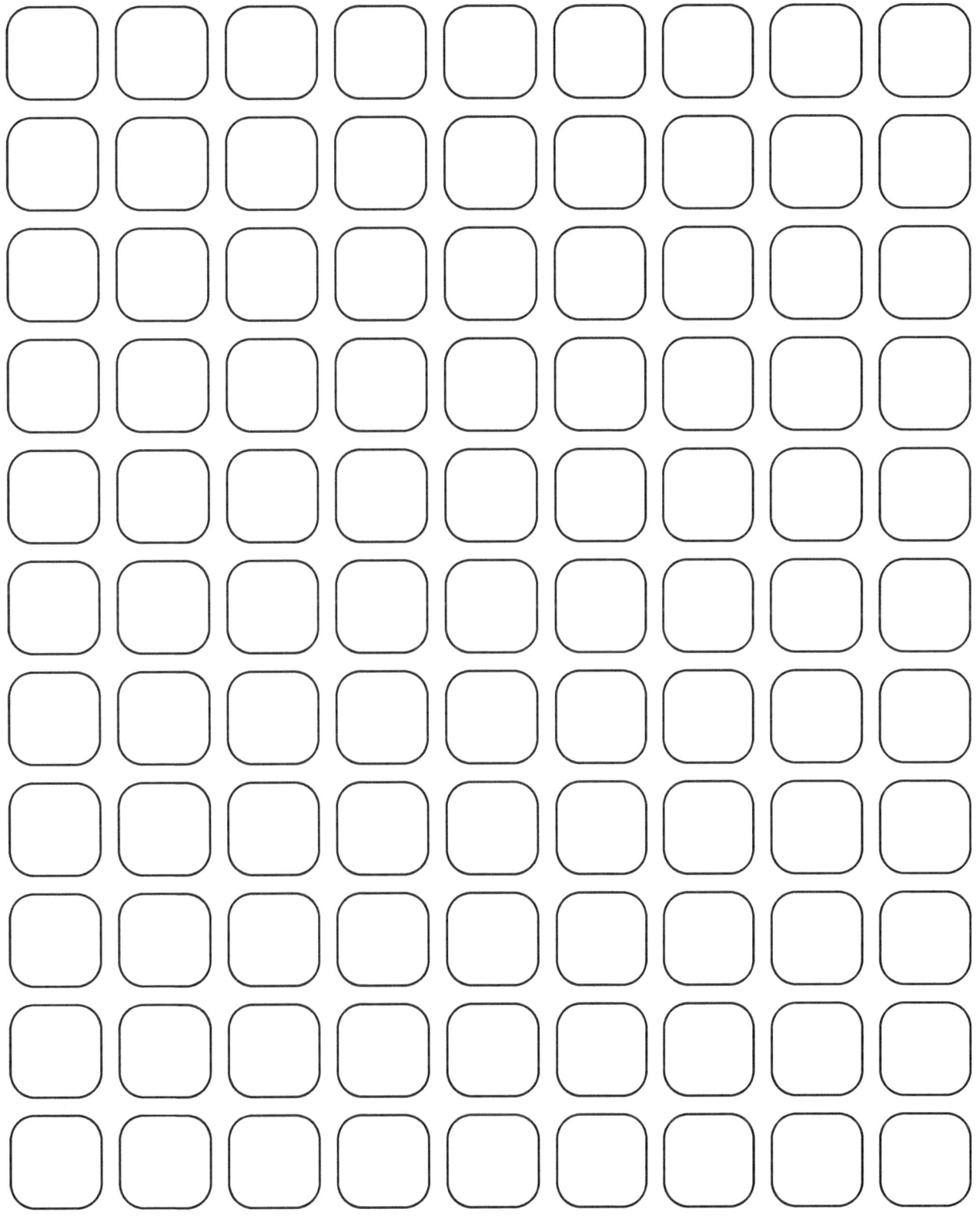

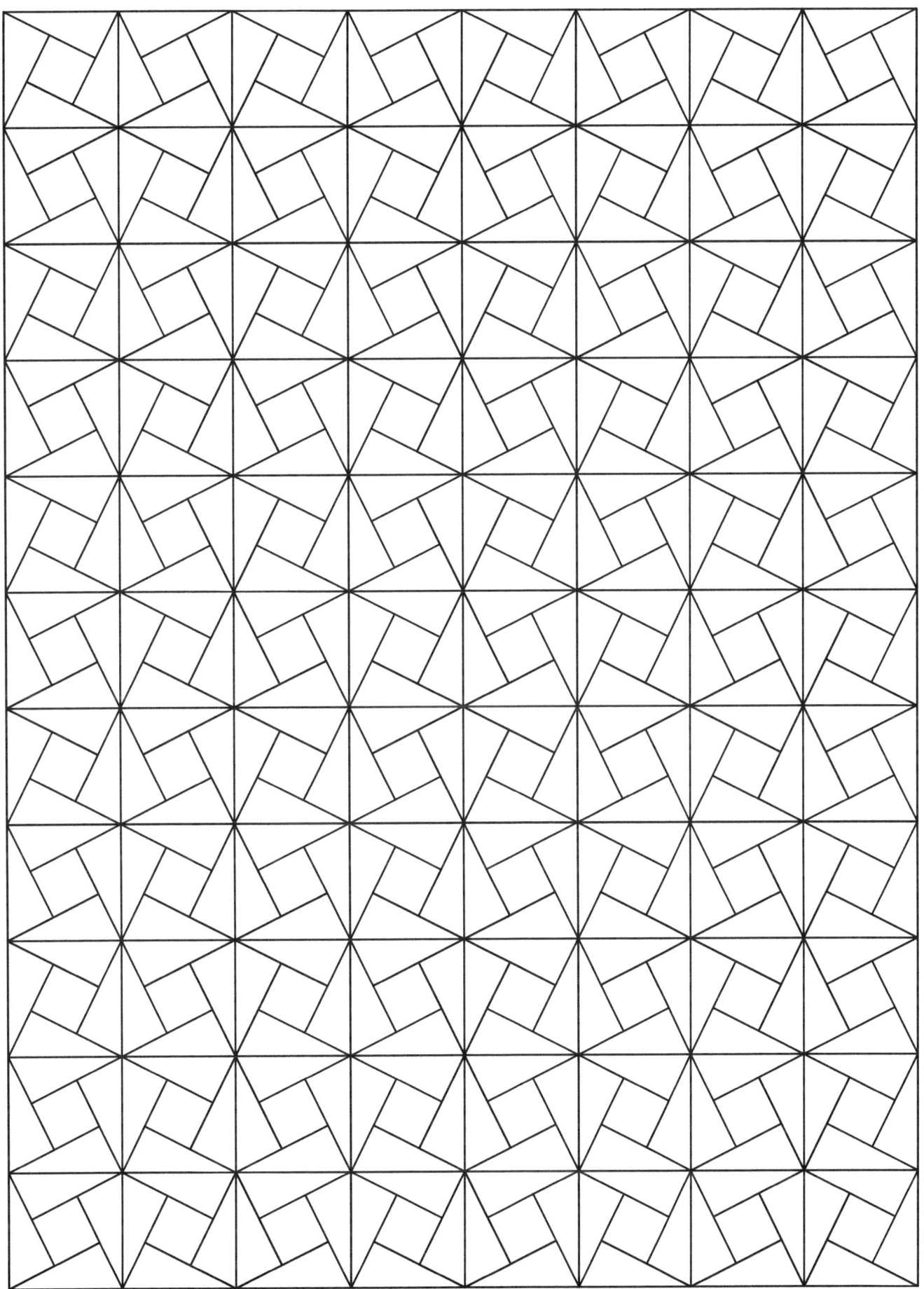

4

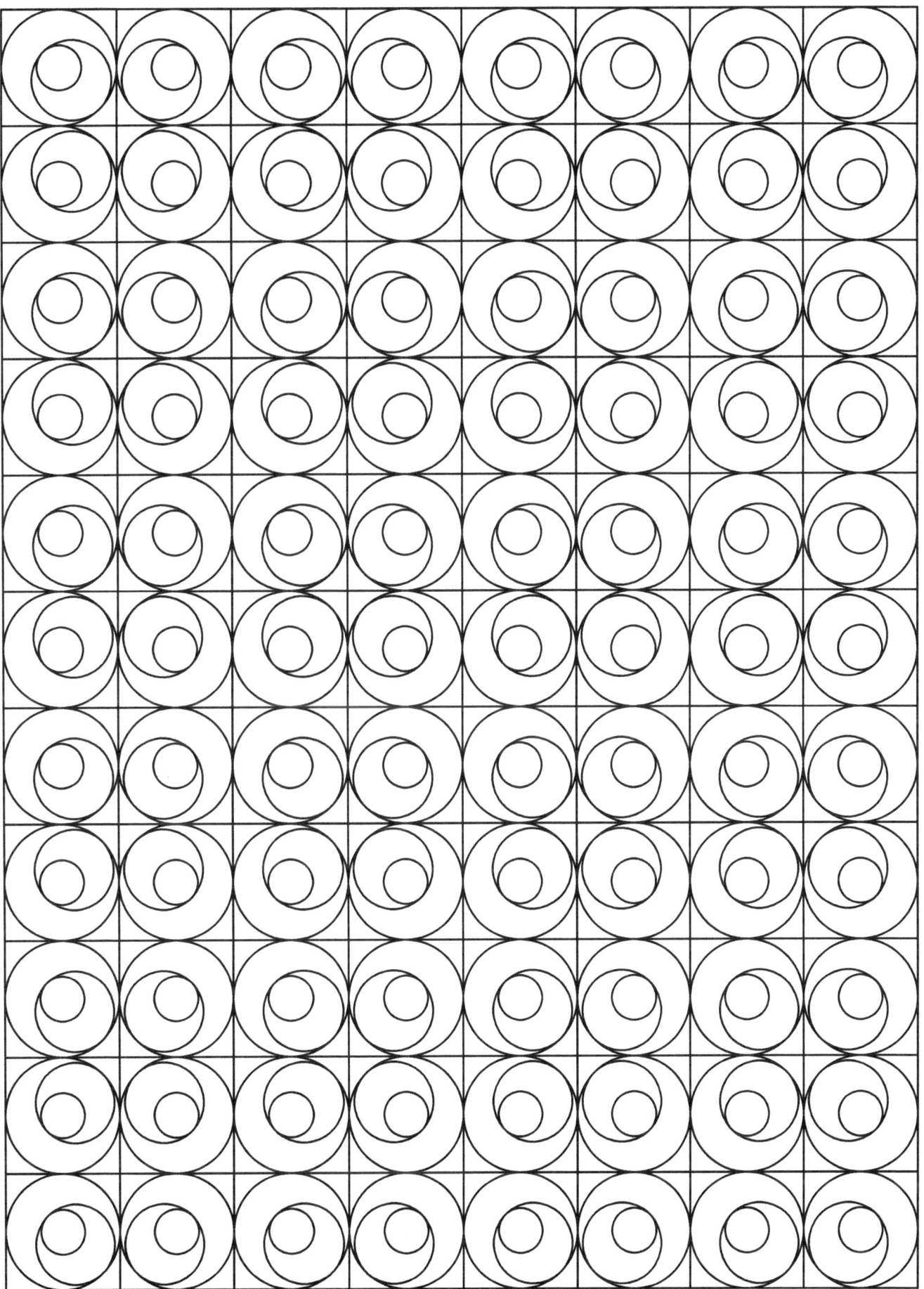

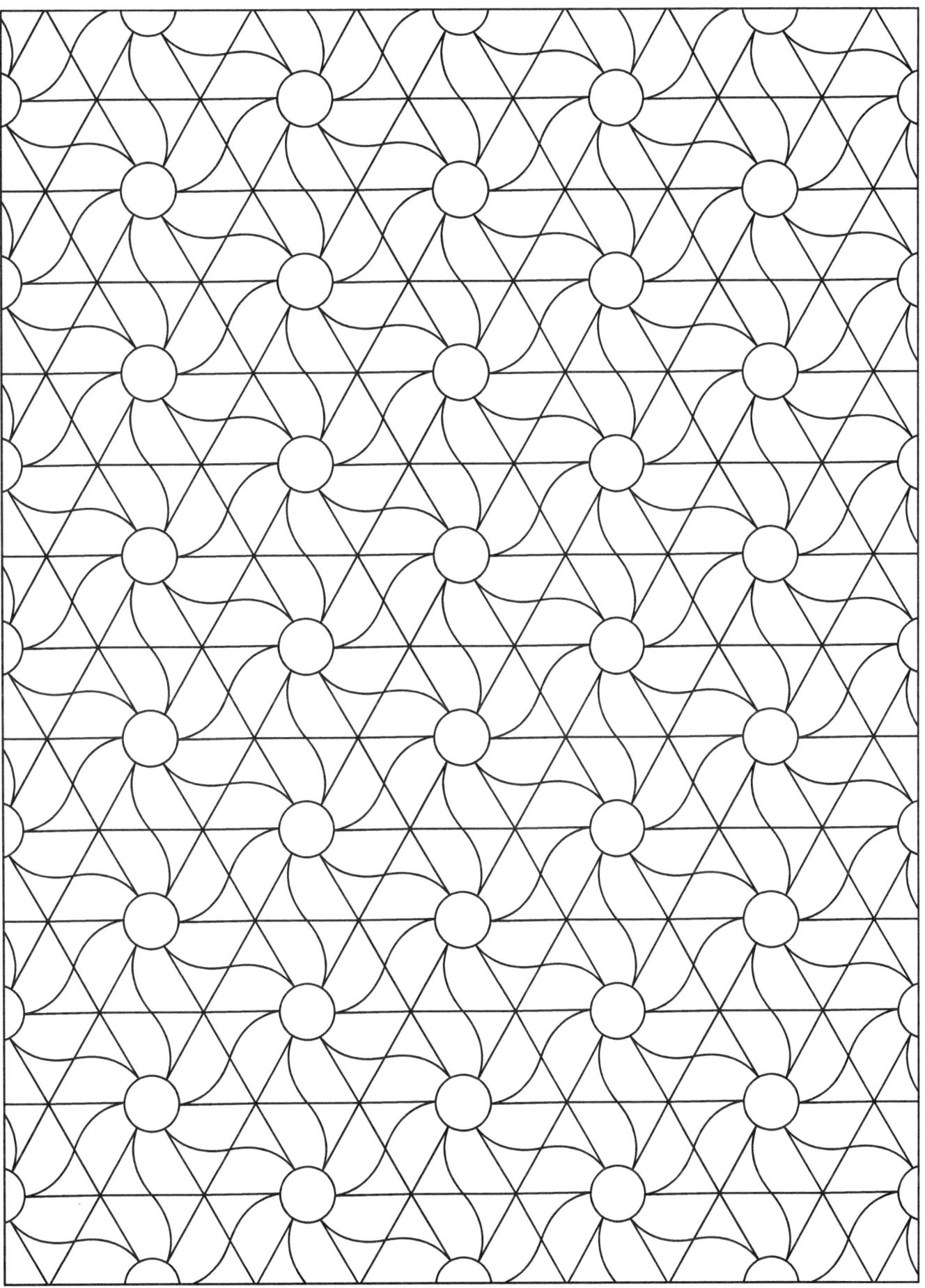

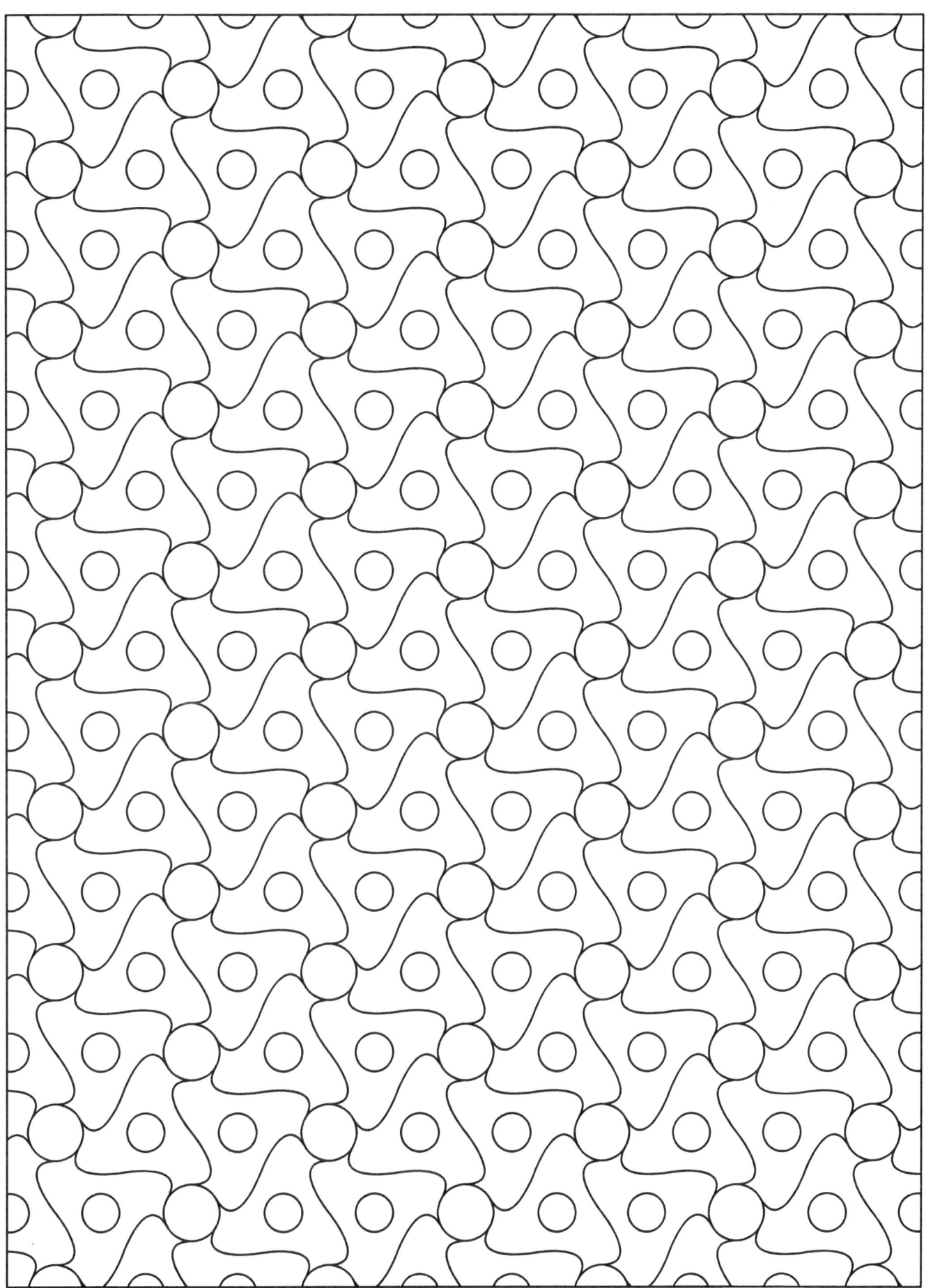

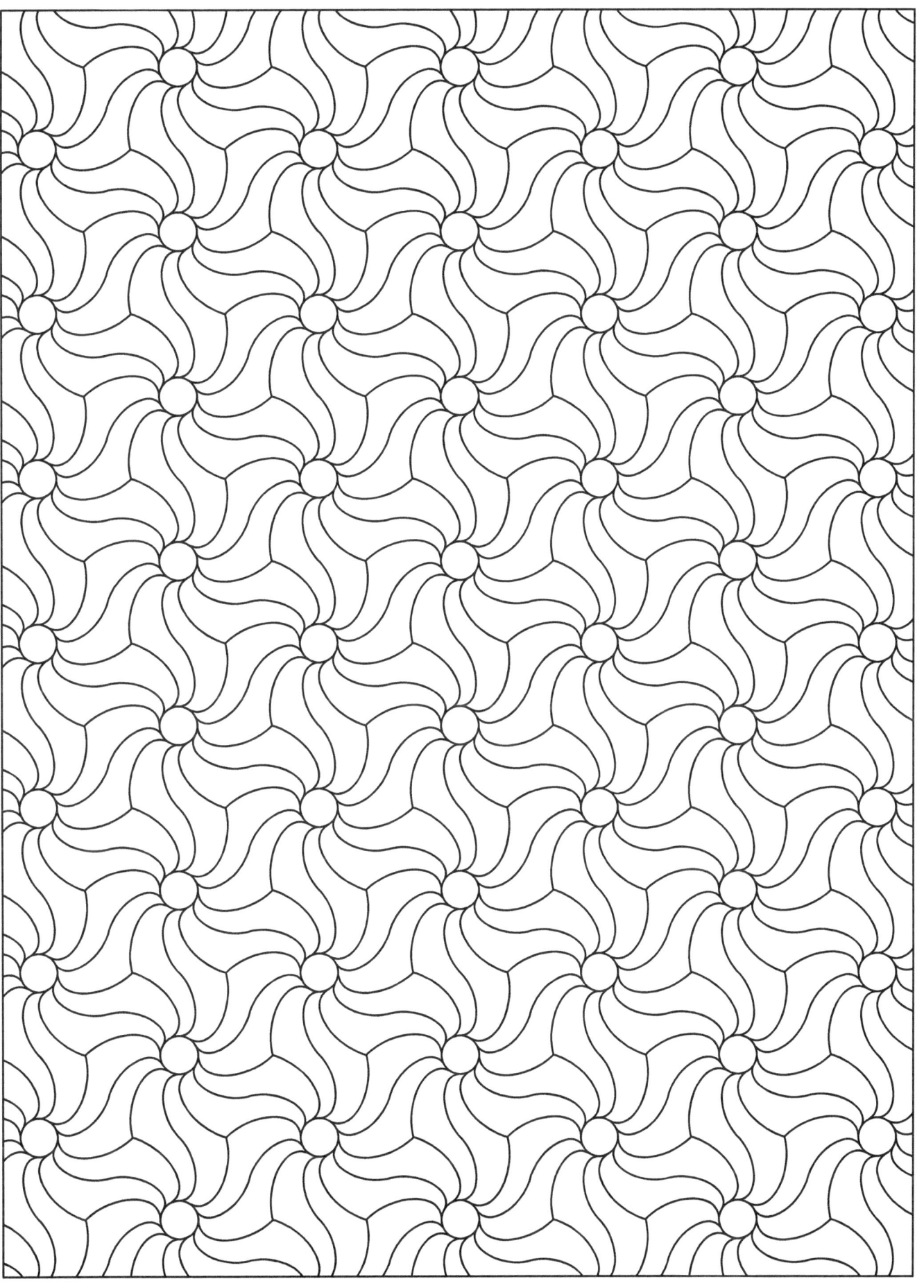

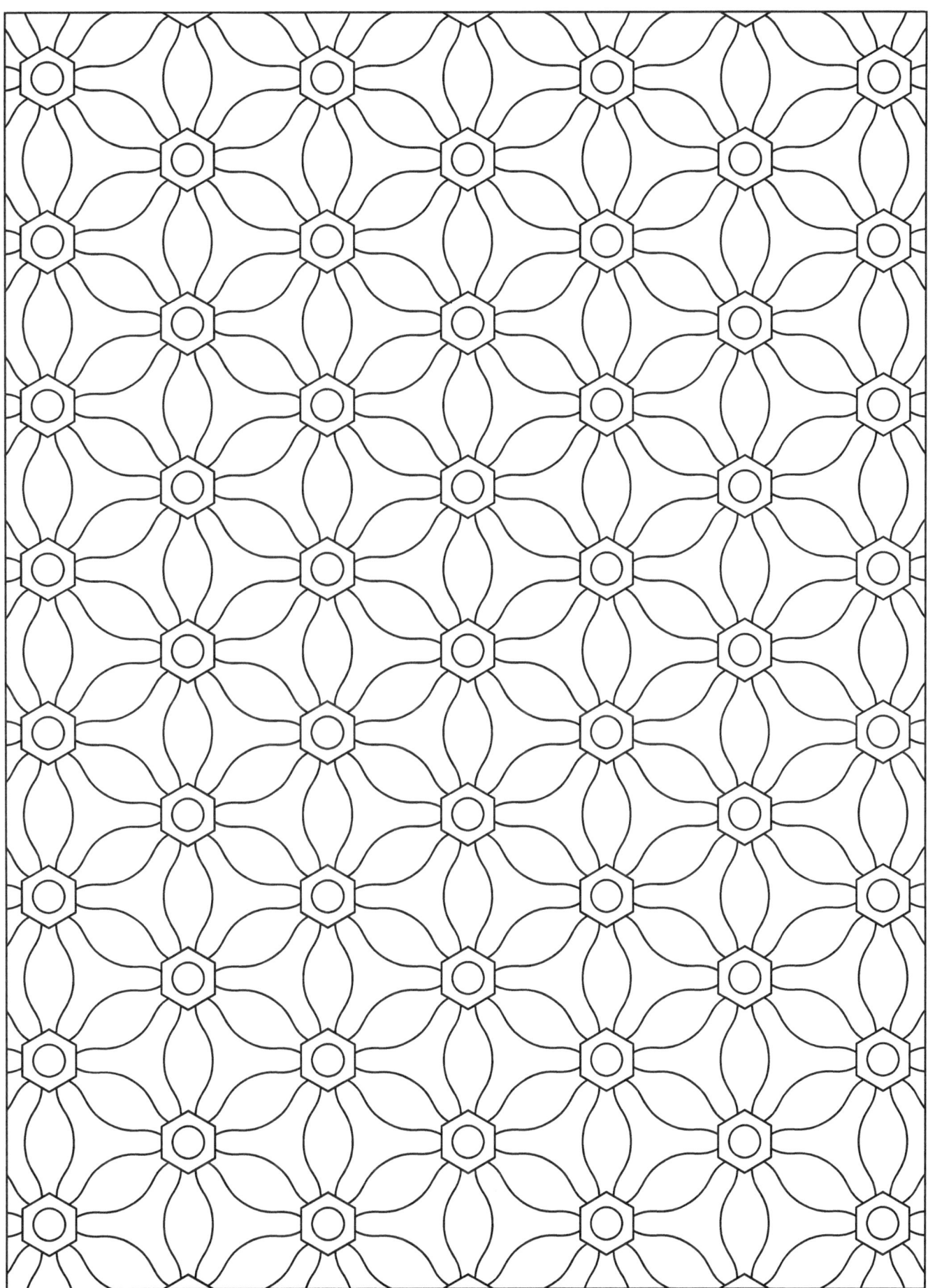

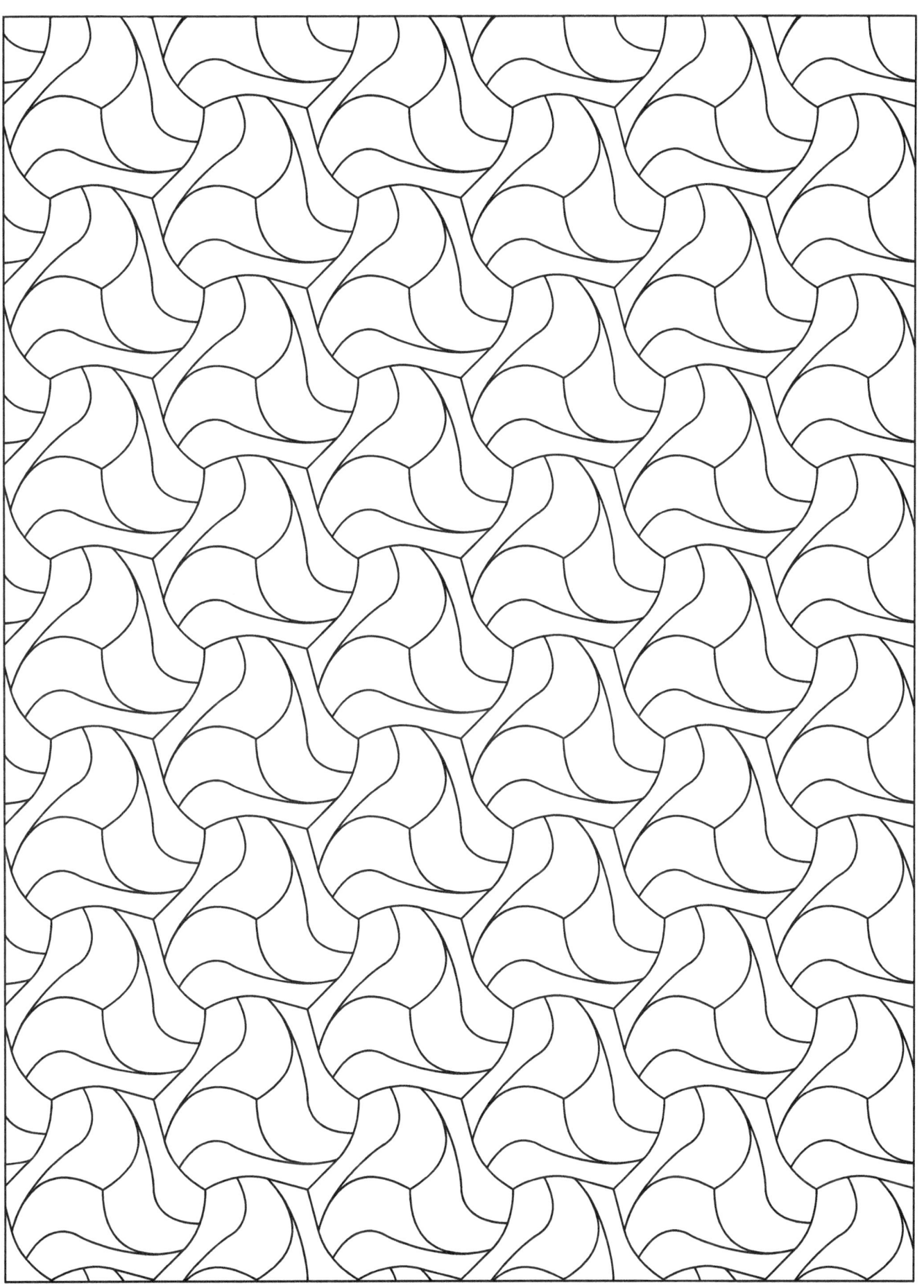

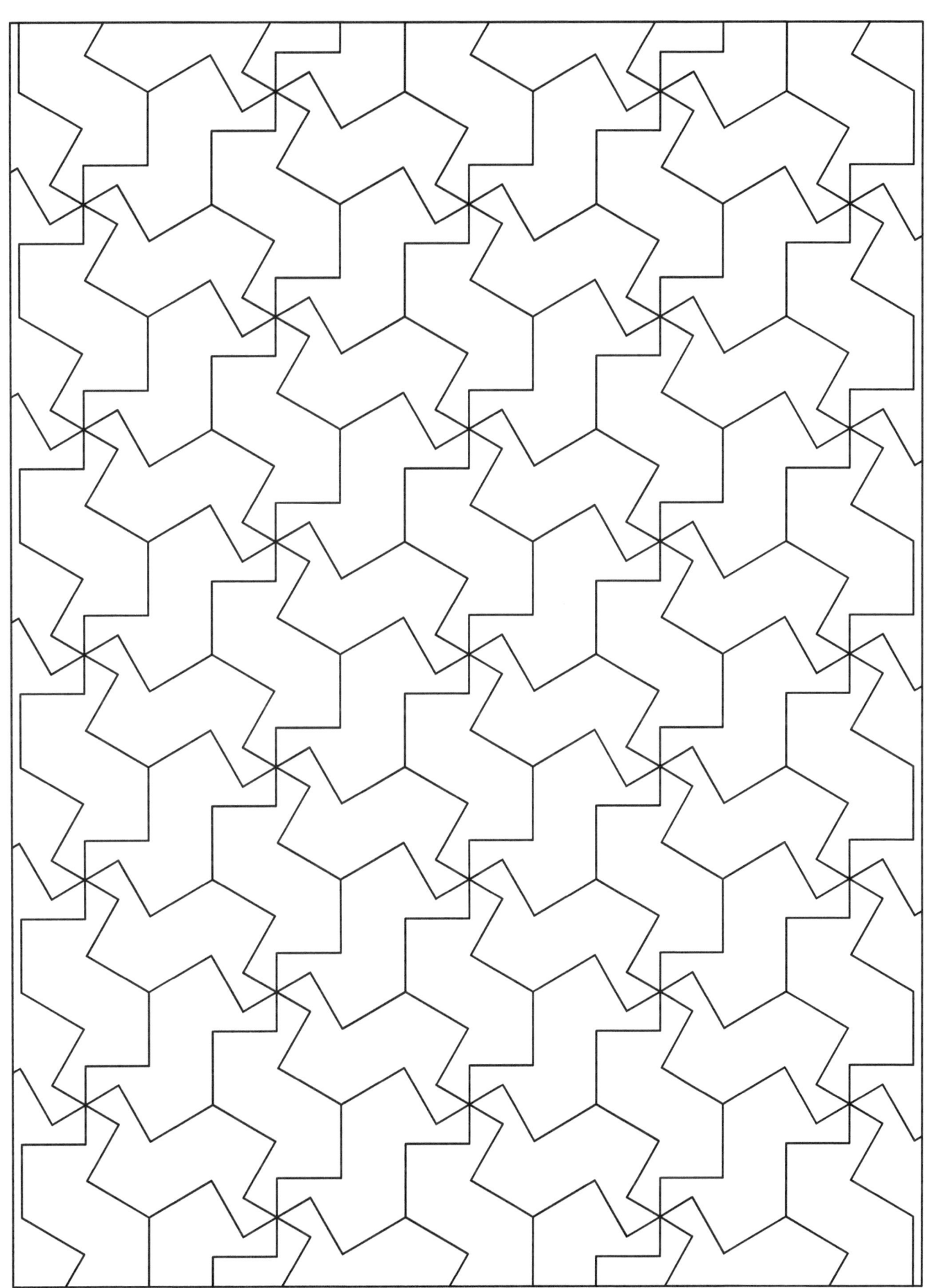

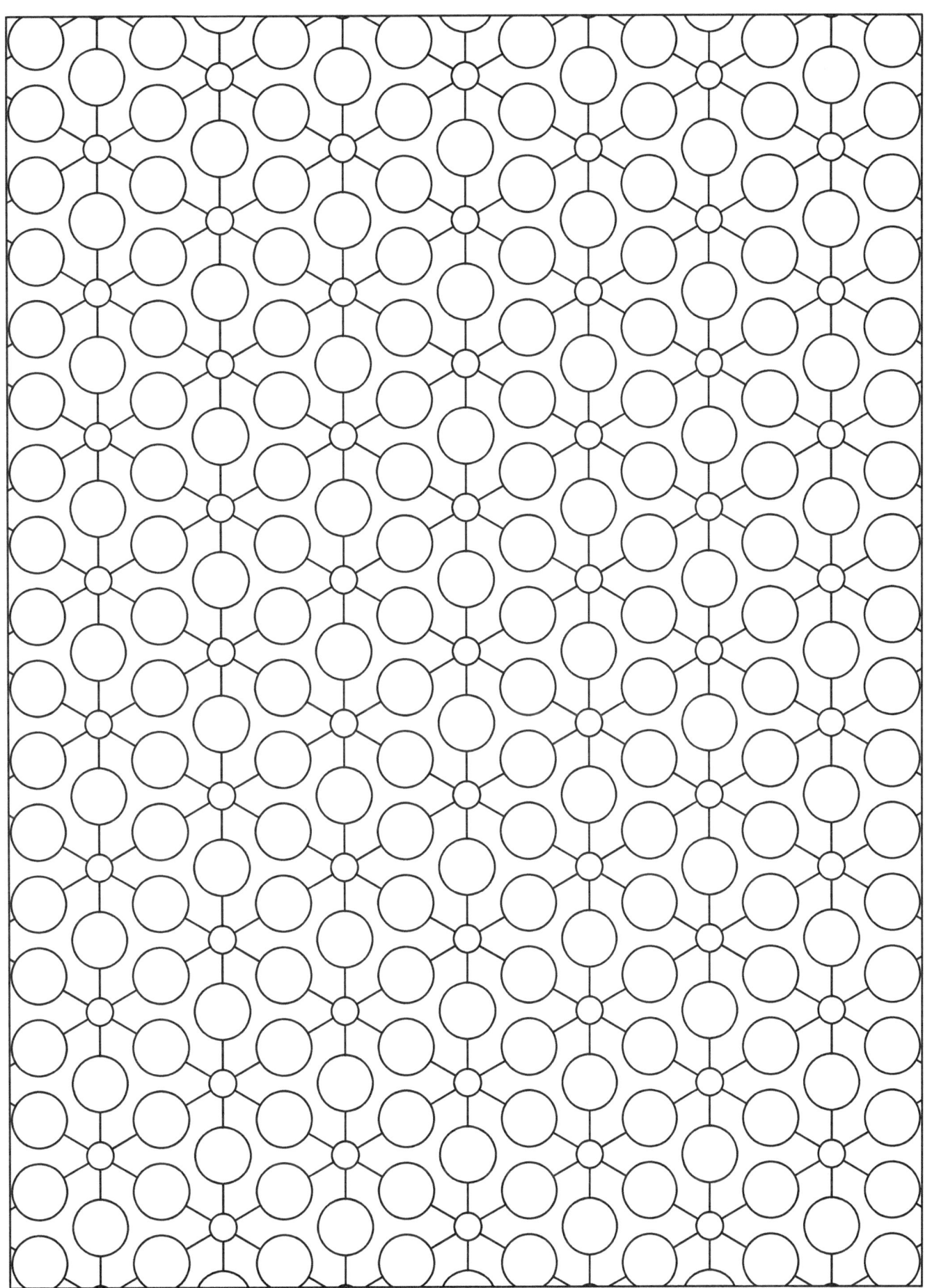

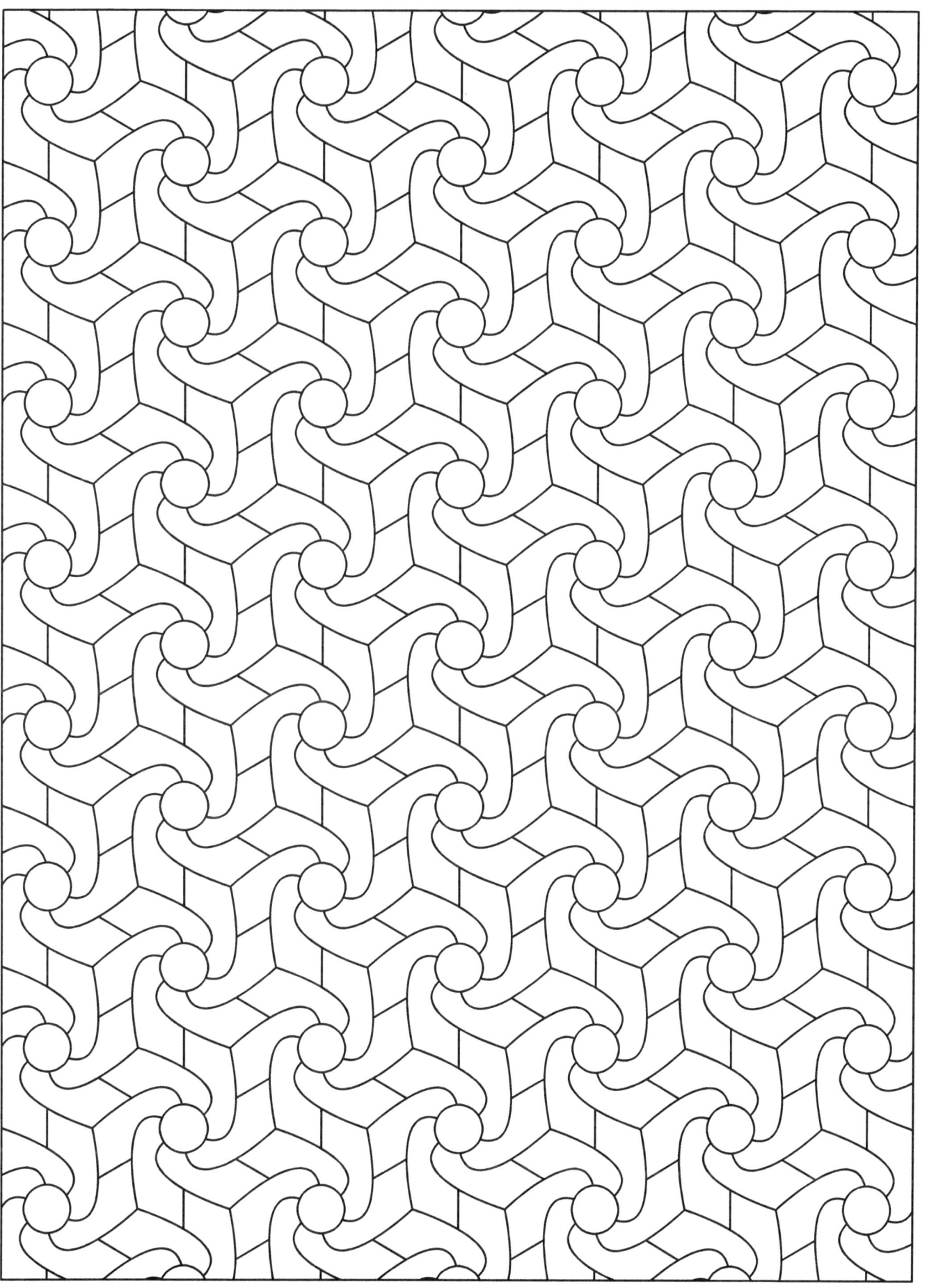

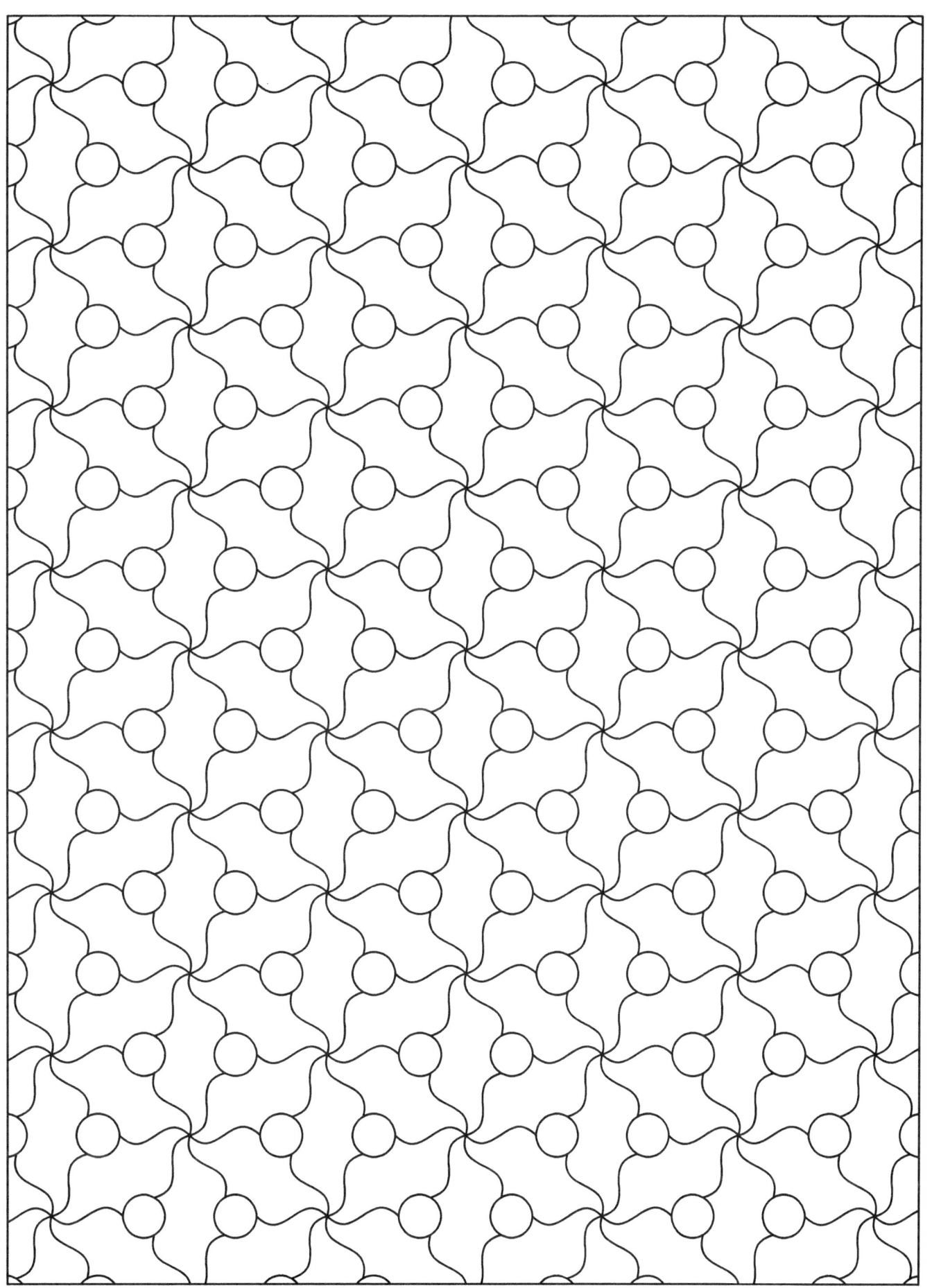

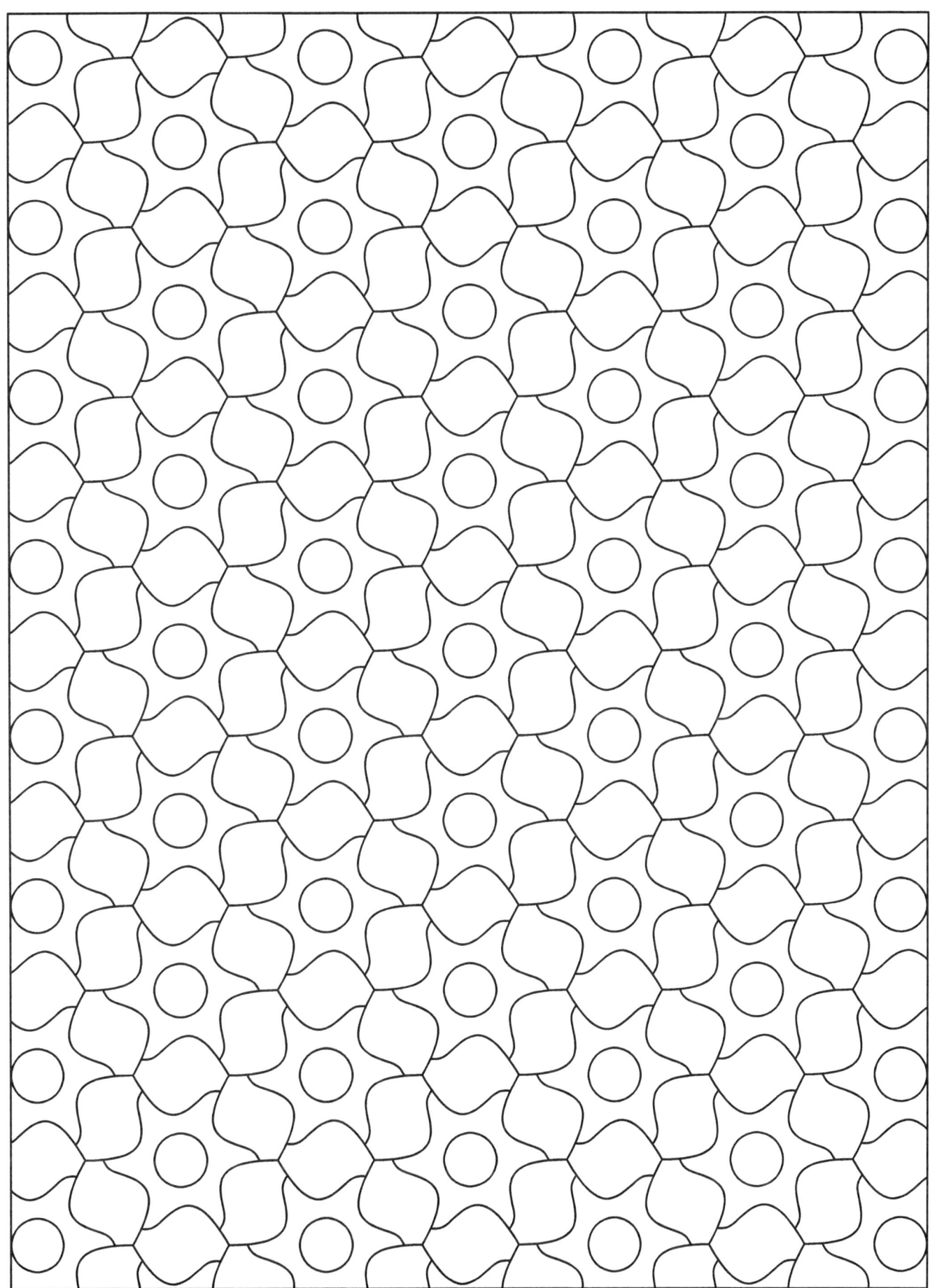

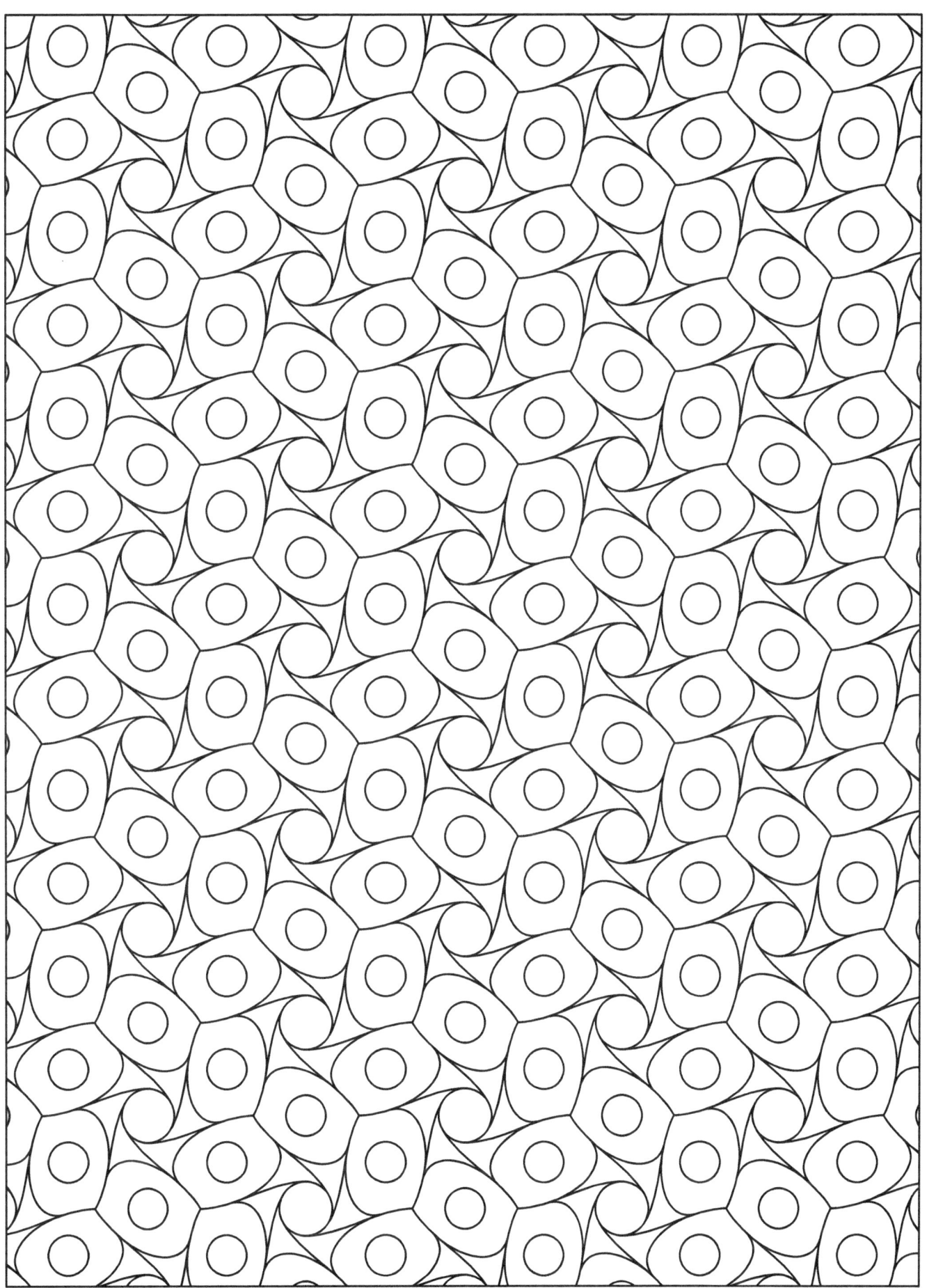

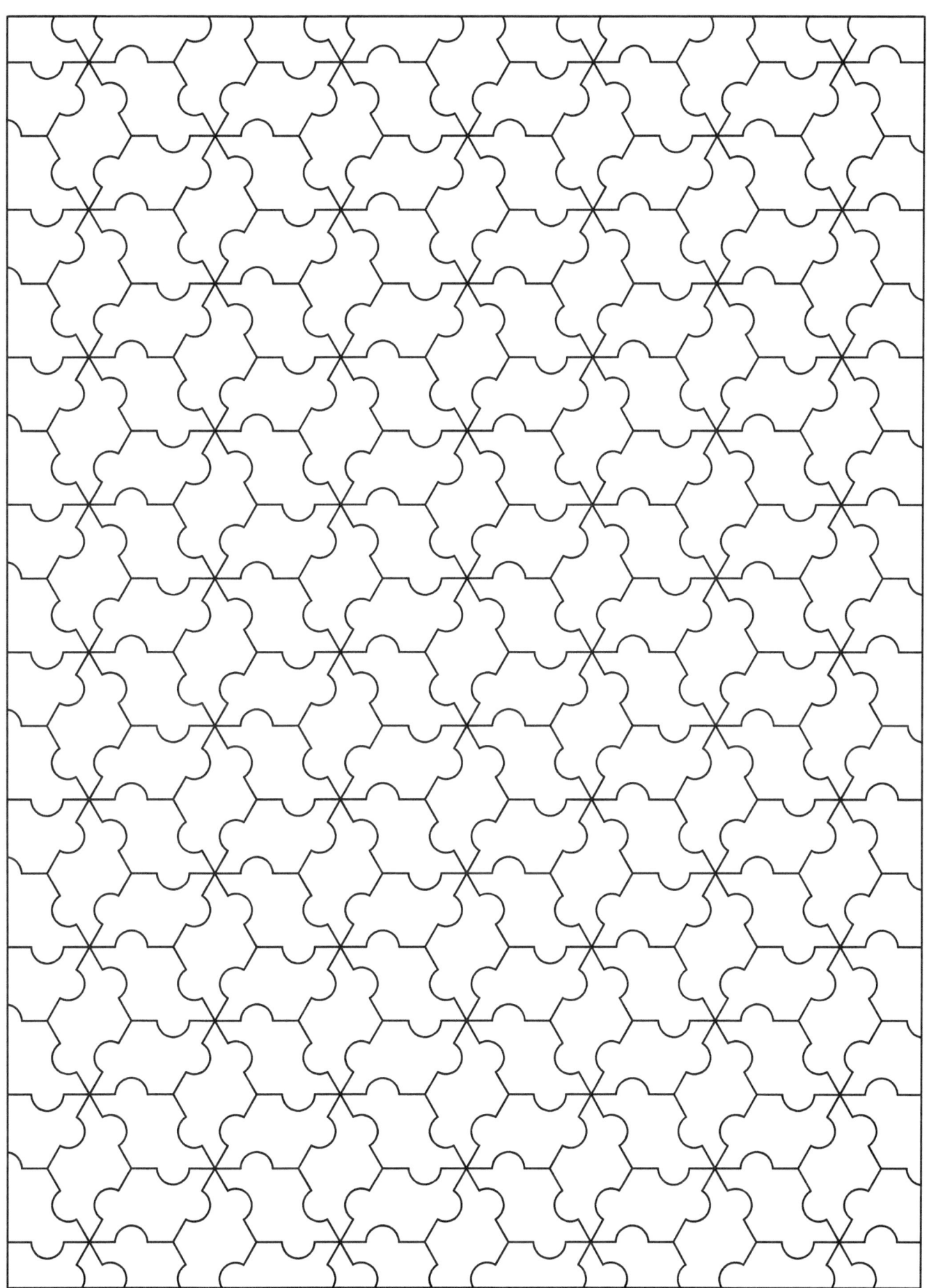

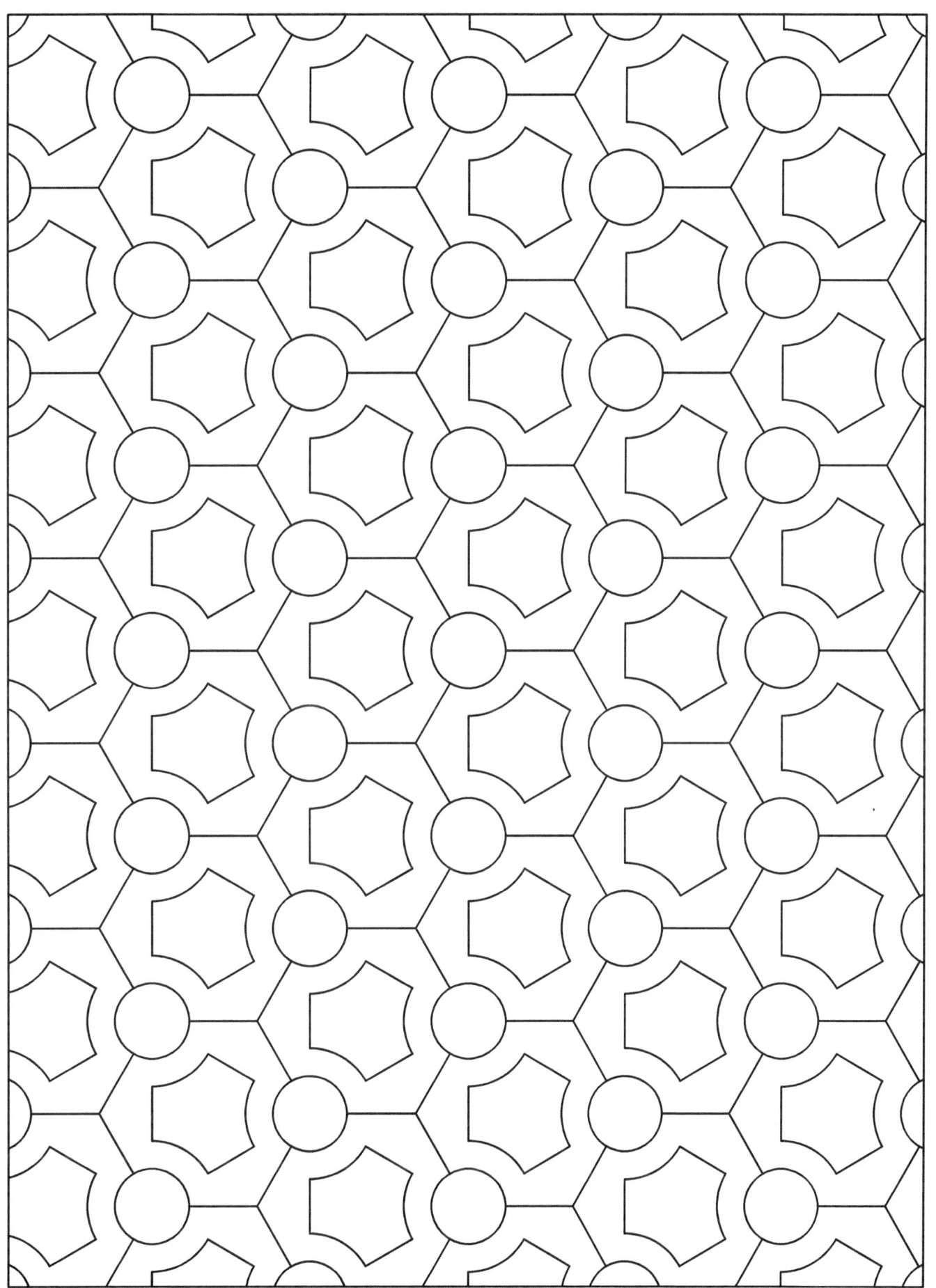

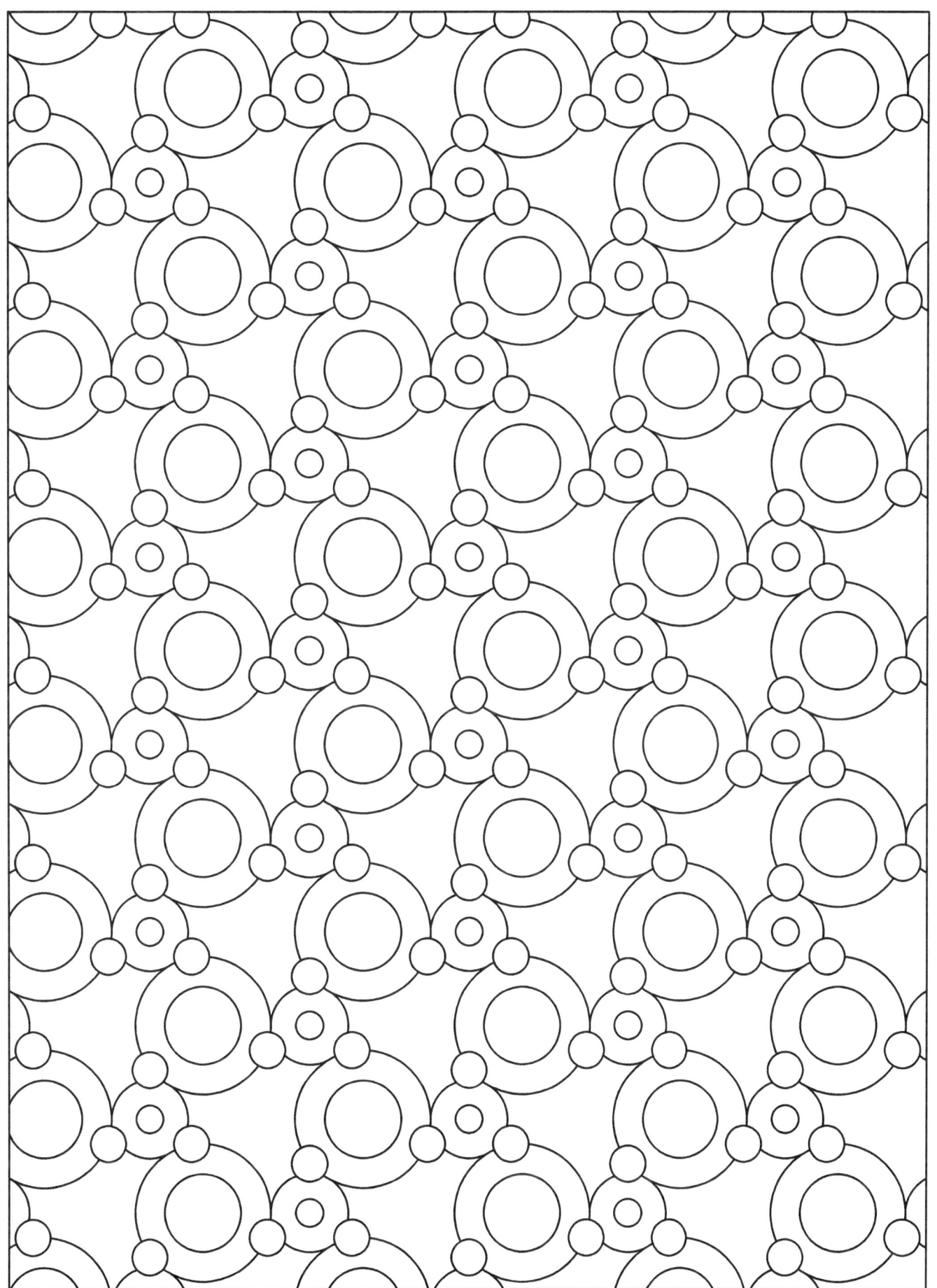

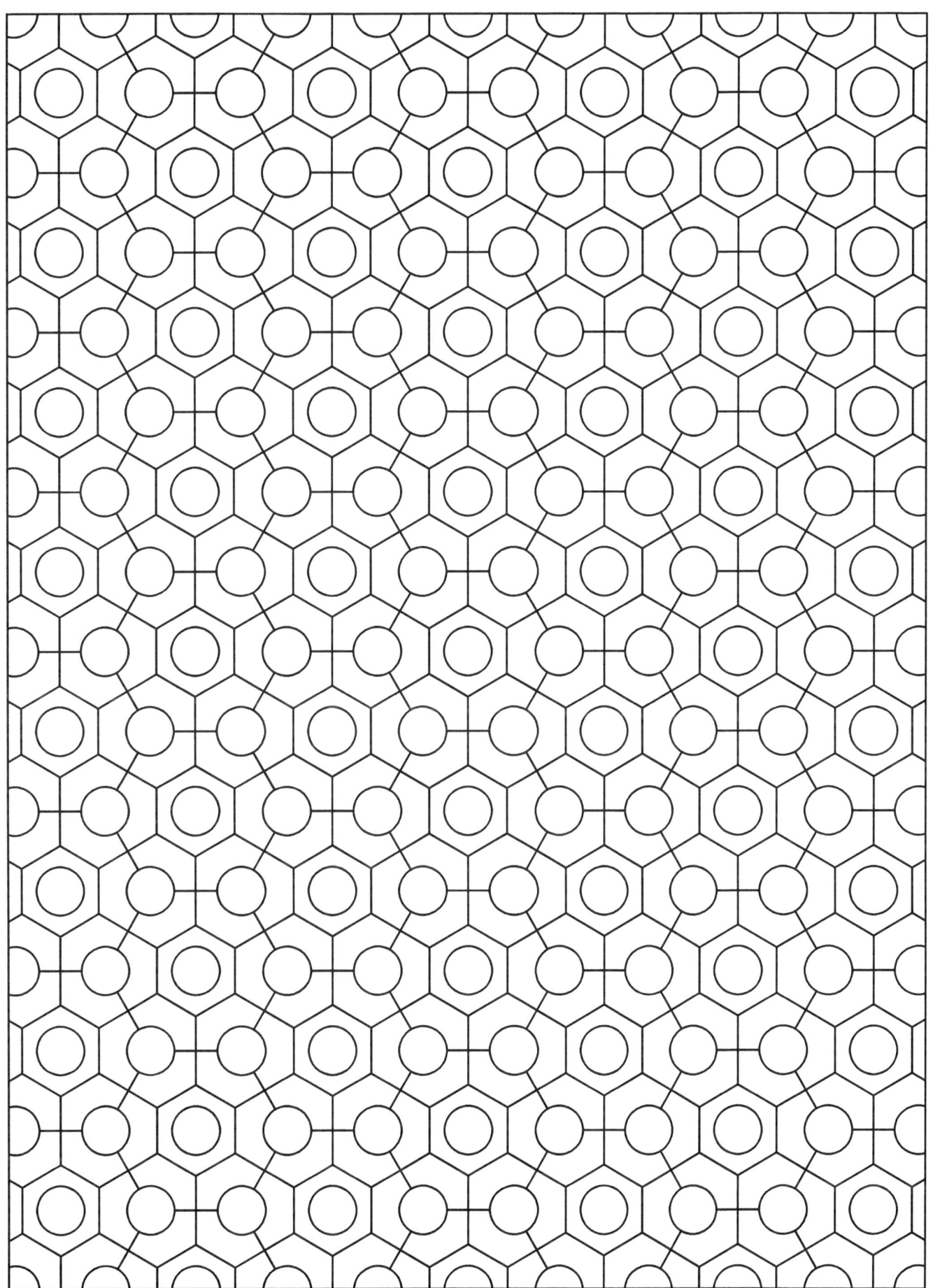

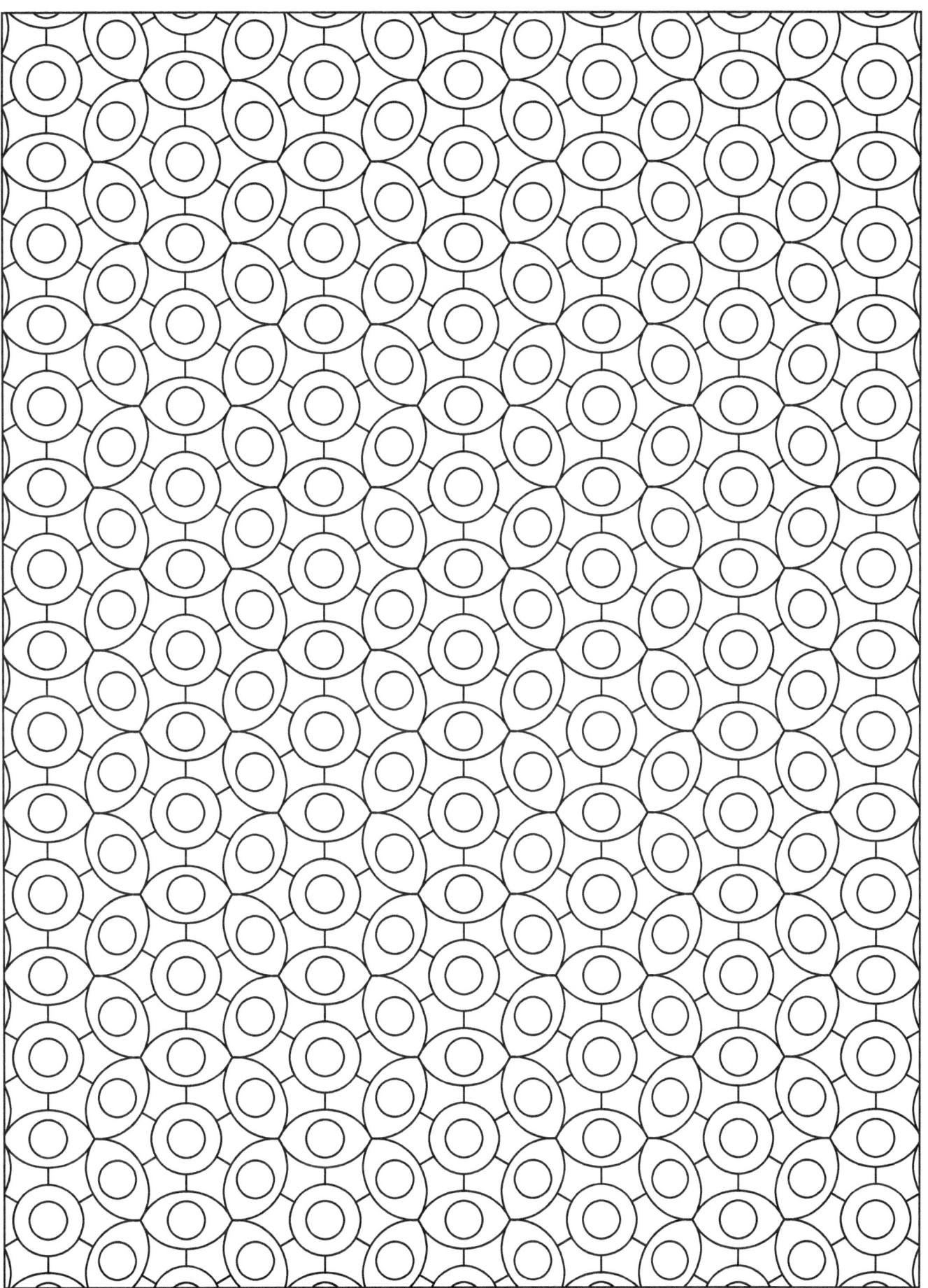

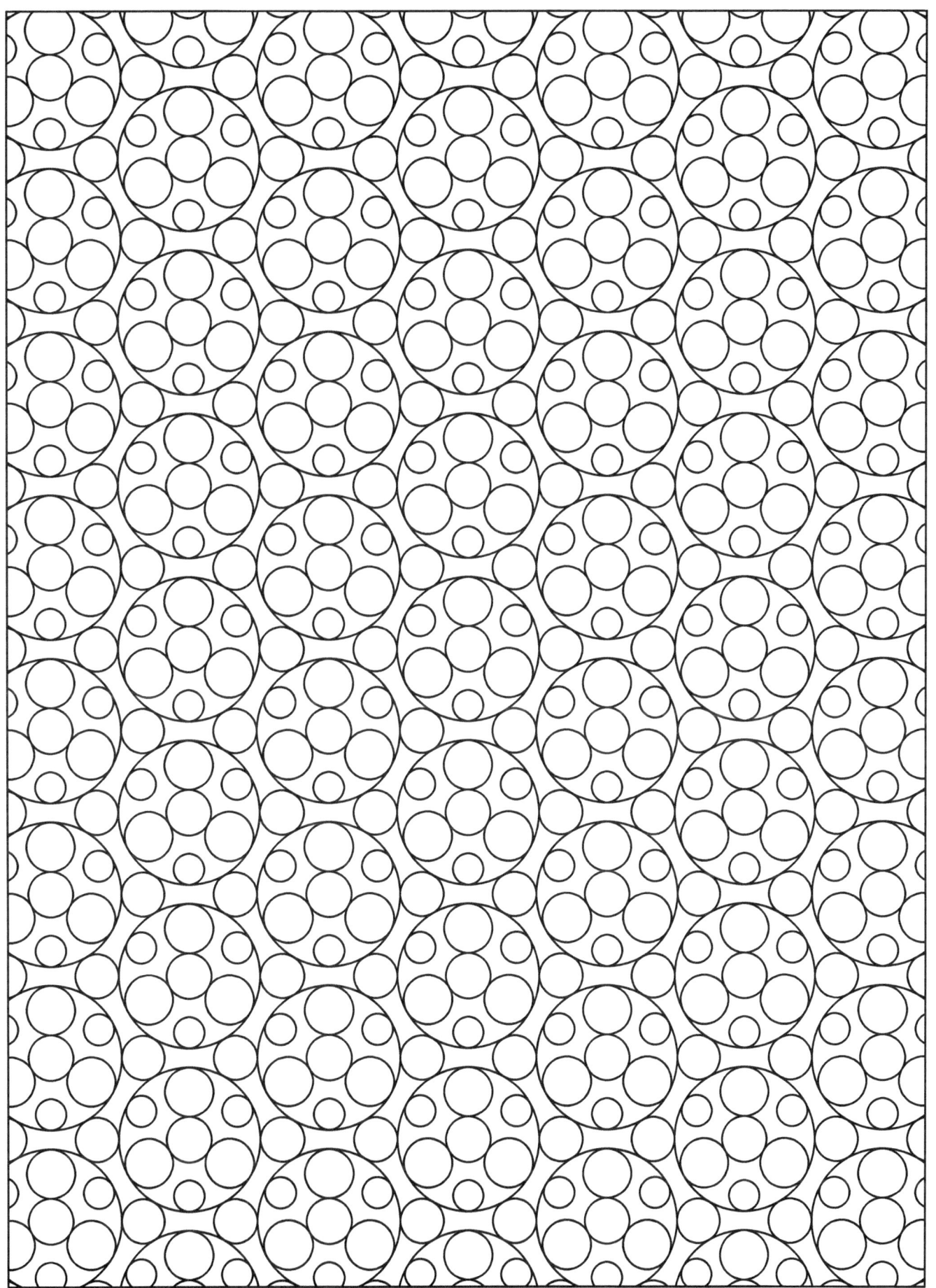

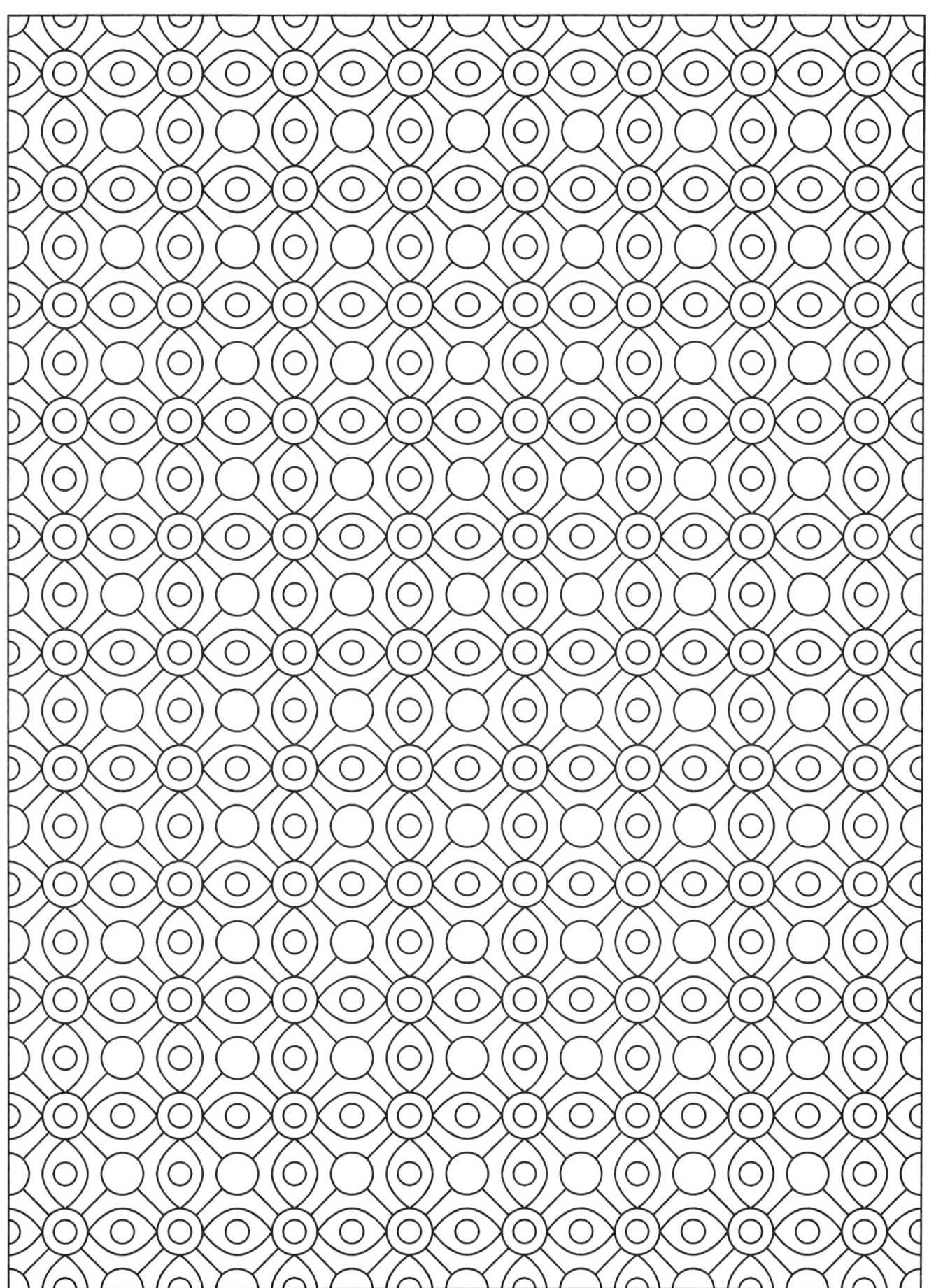

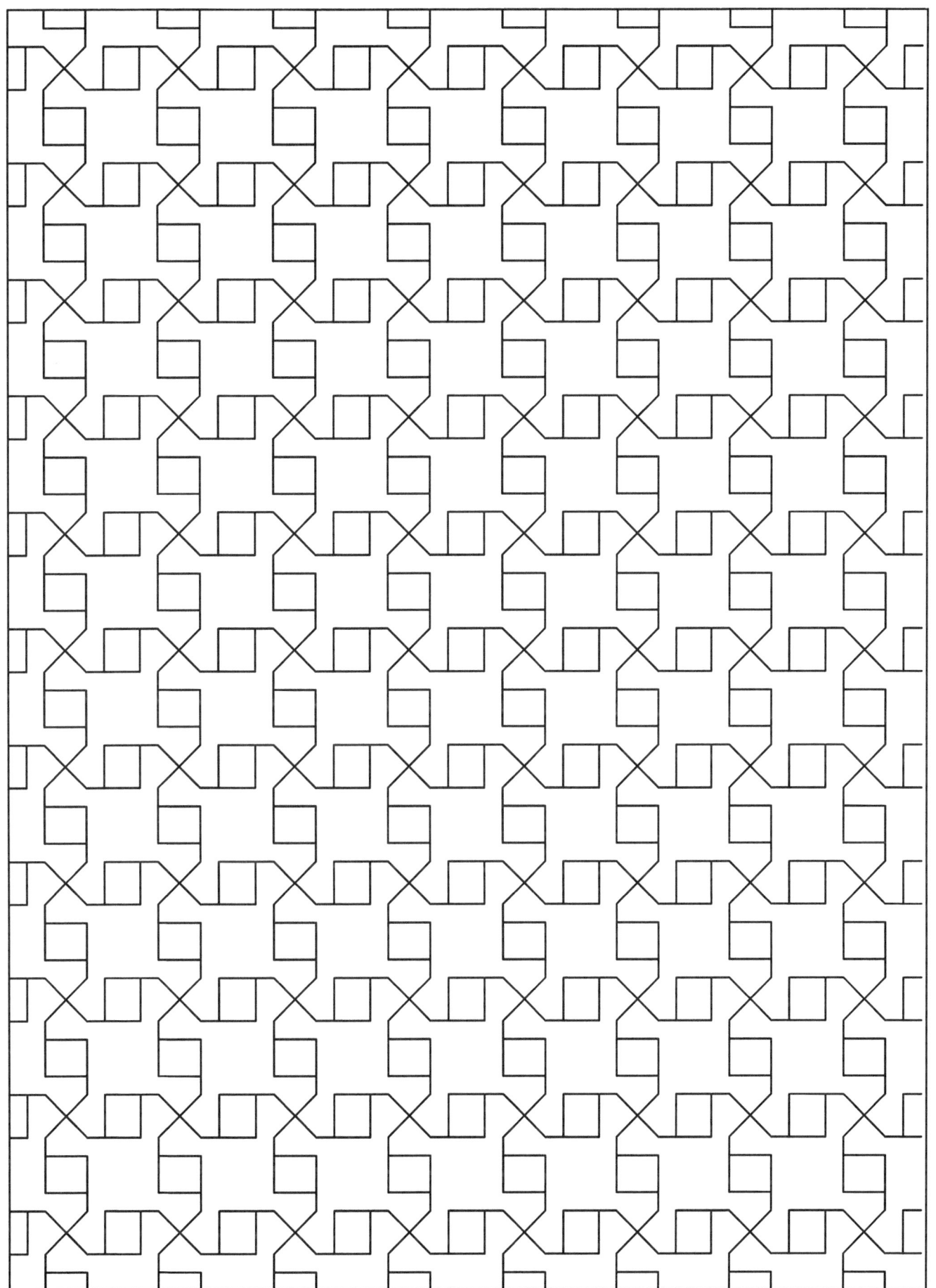

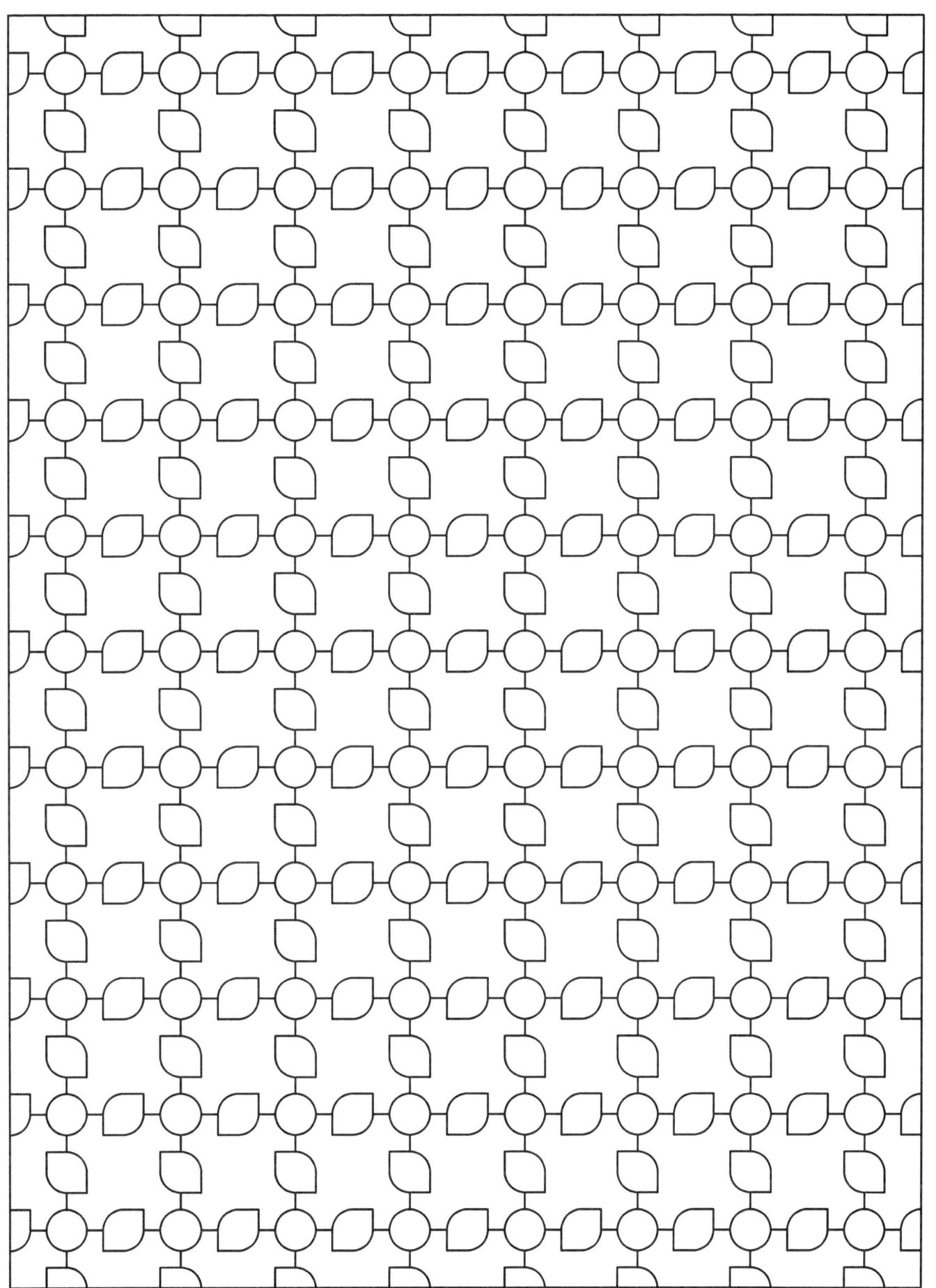

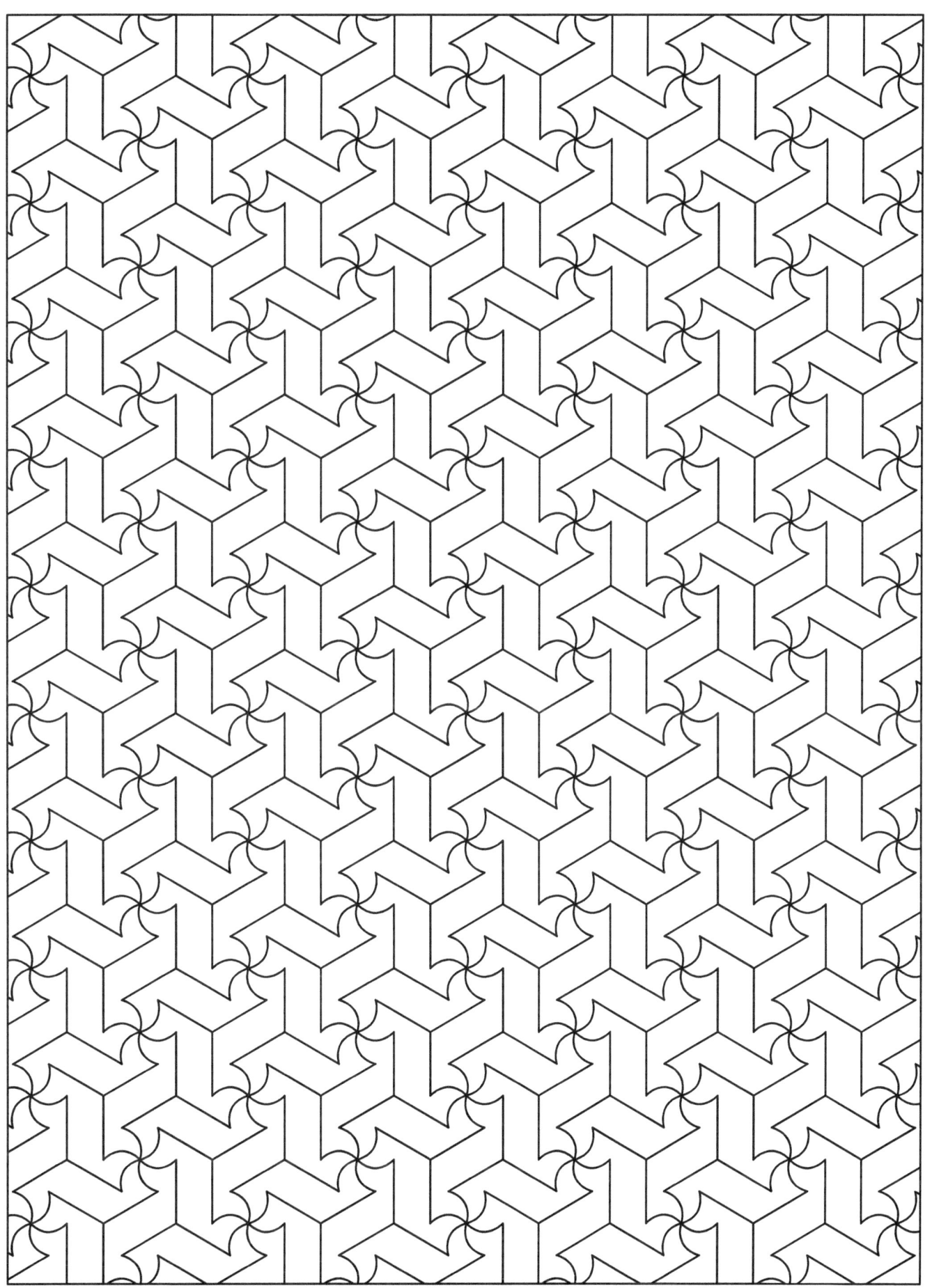

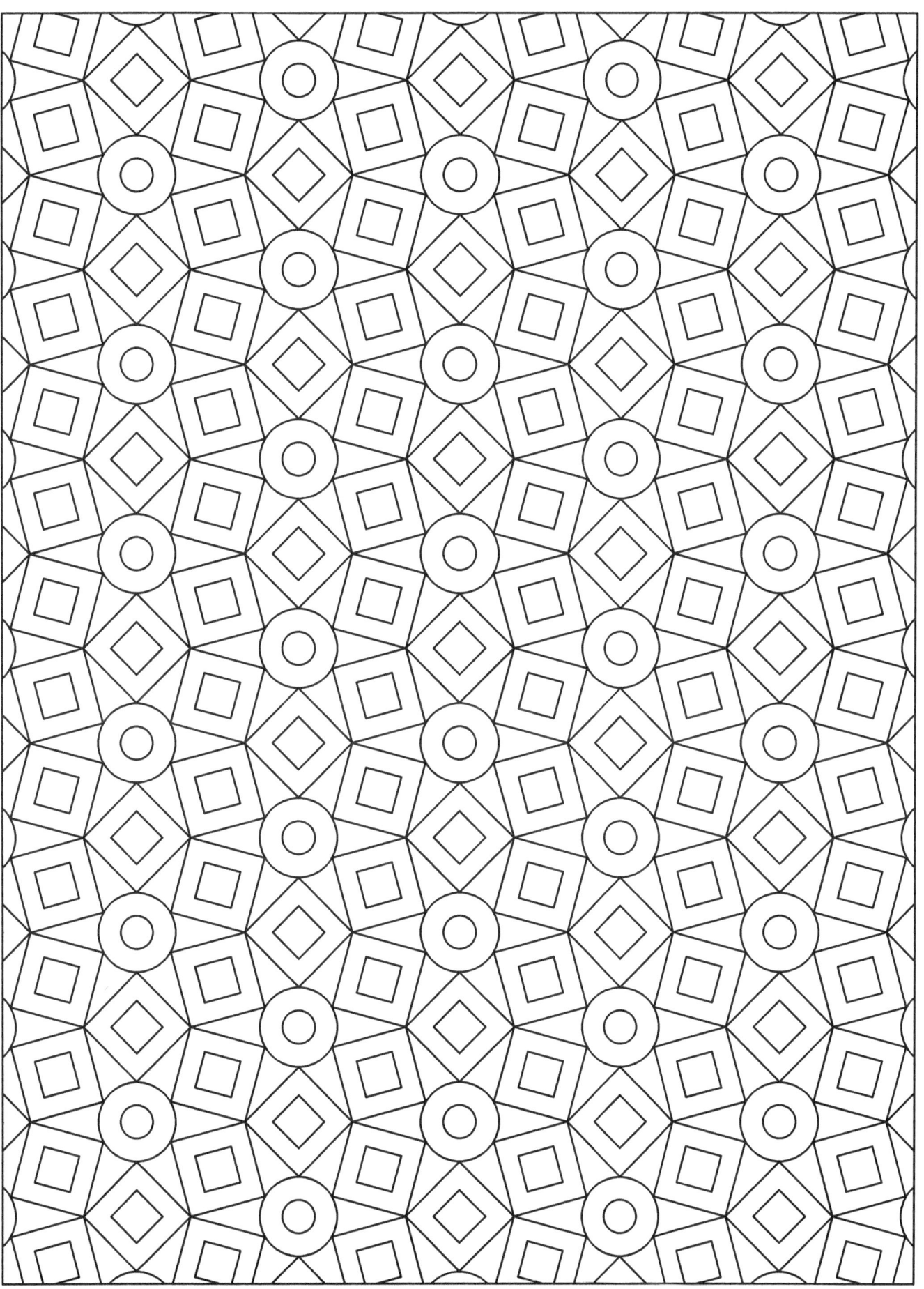

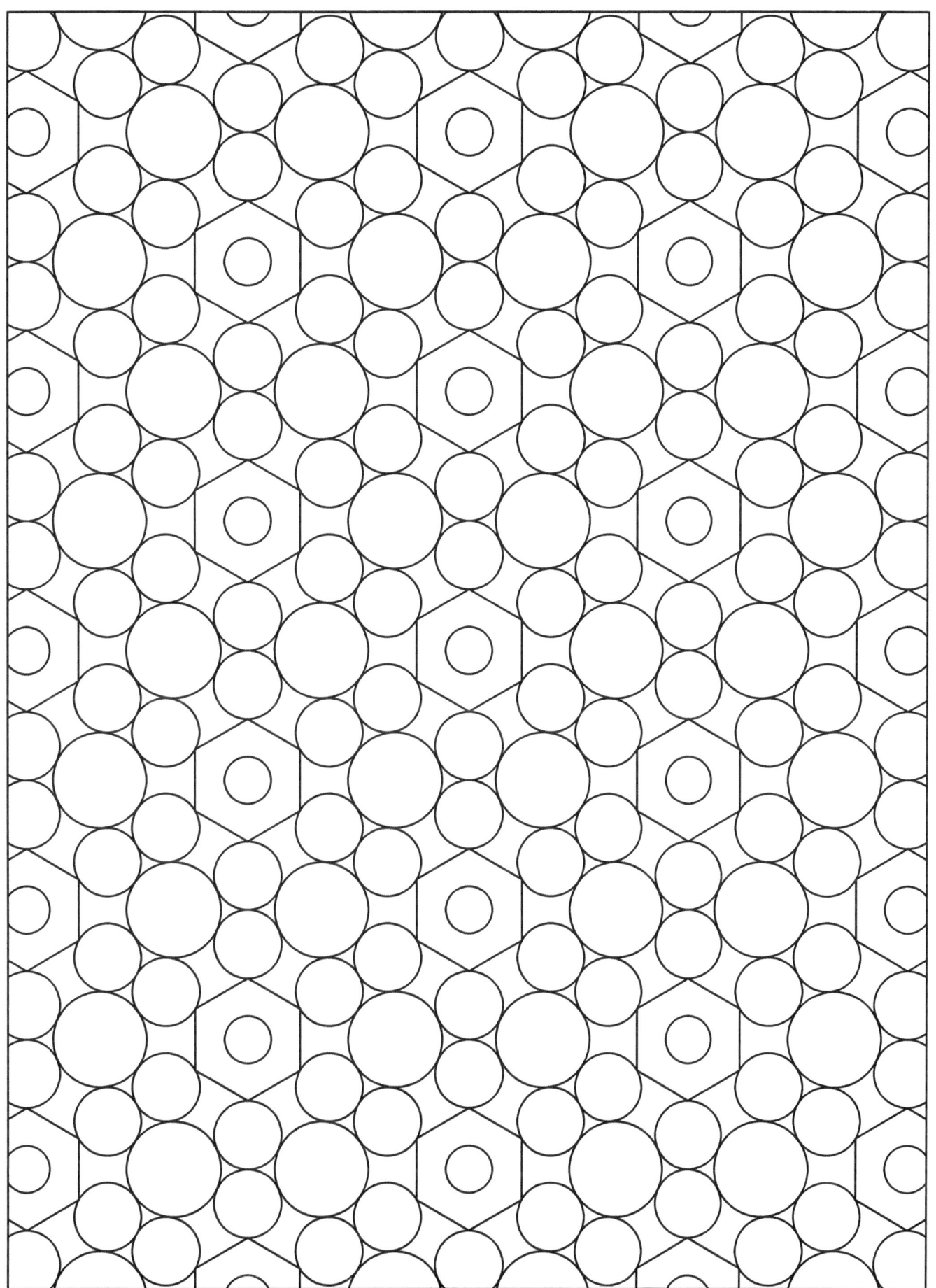

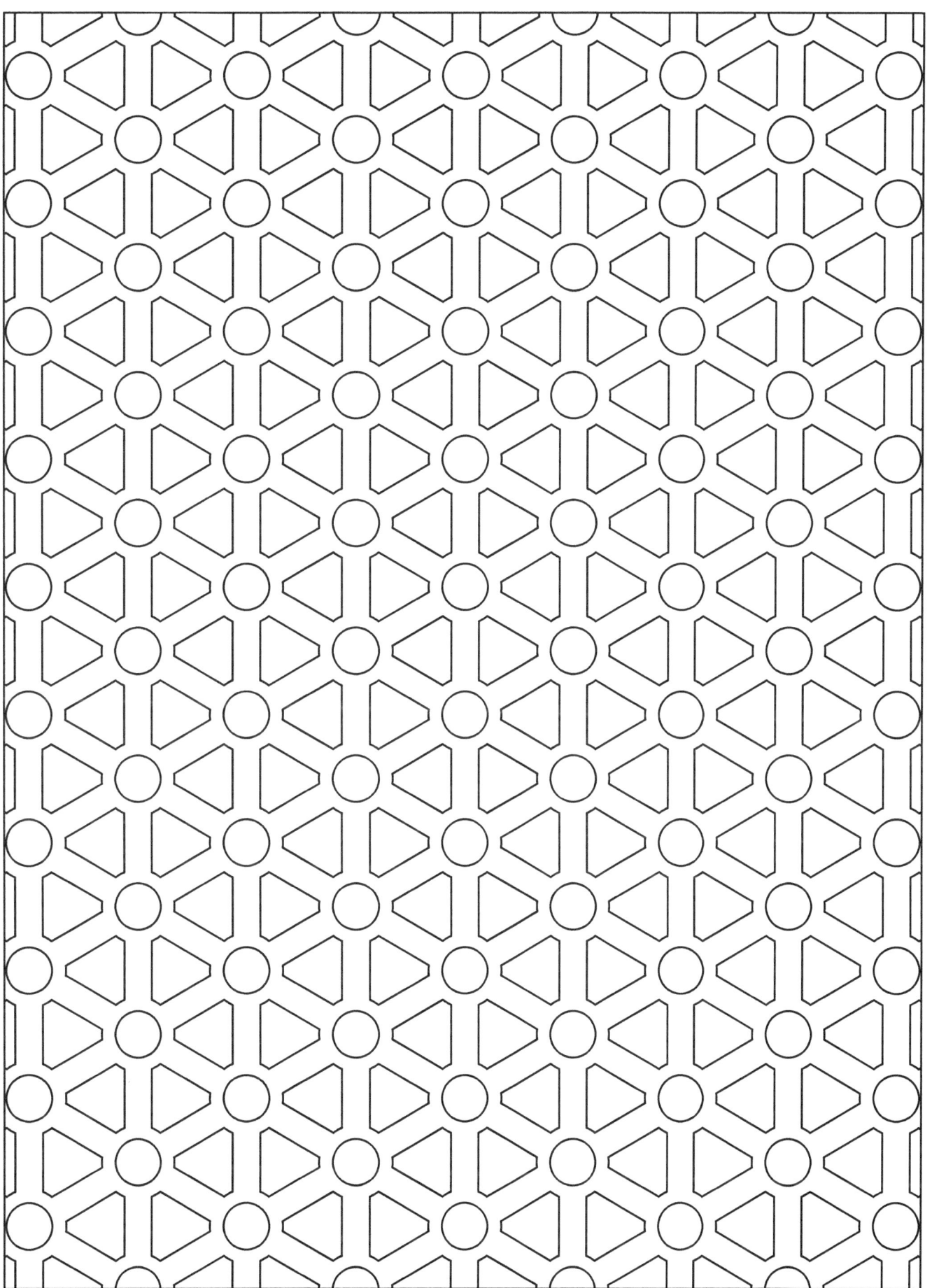

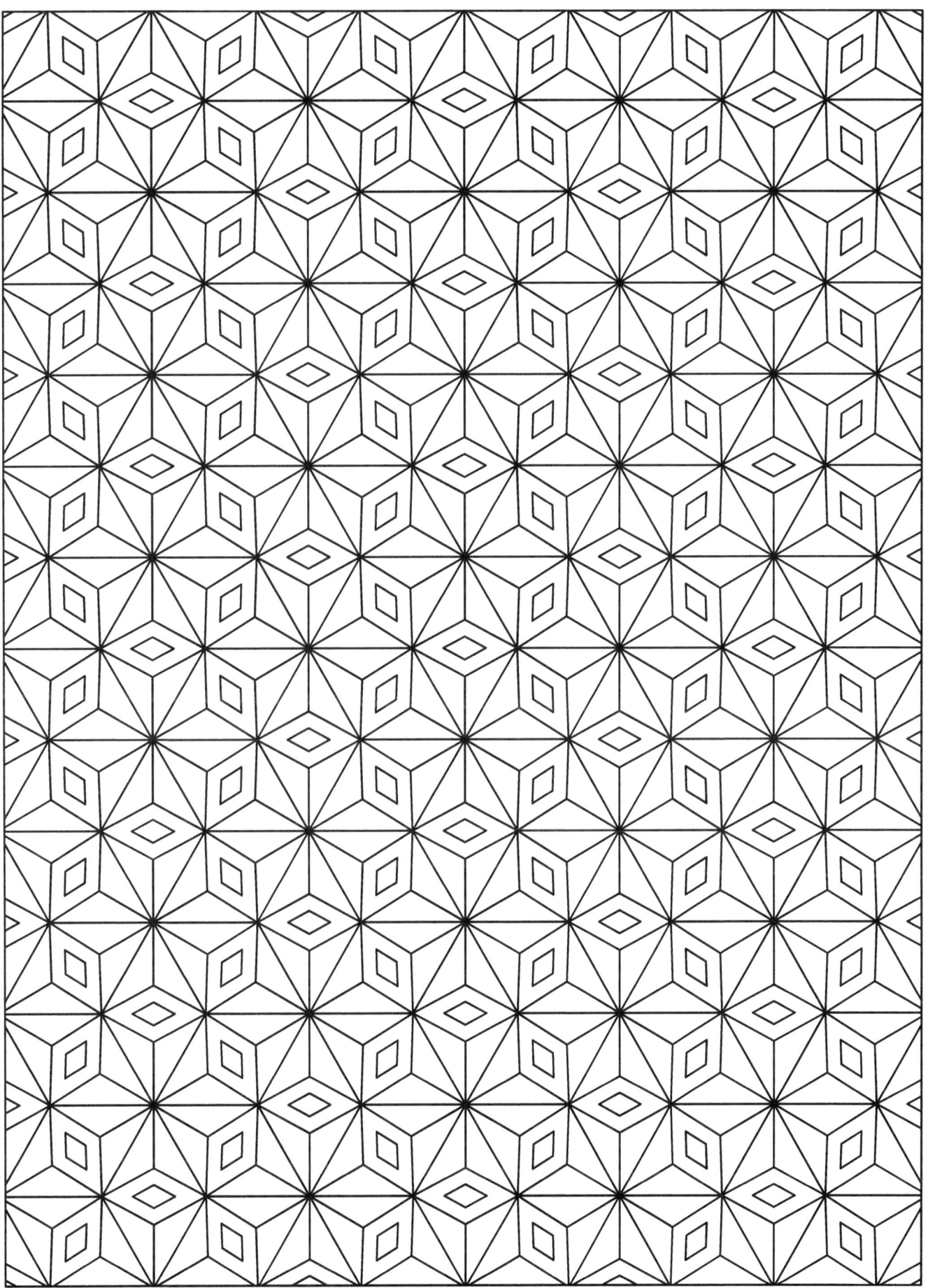

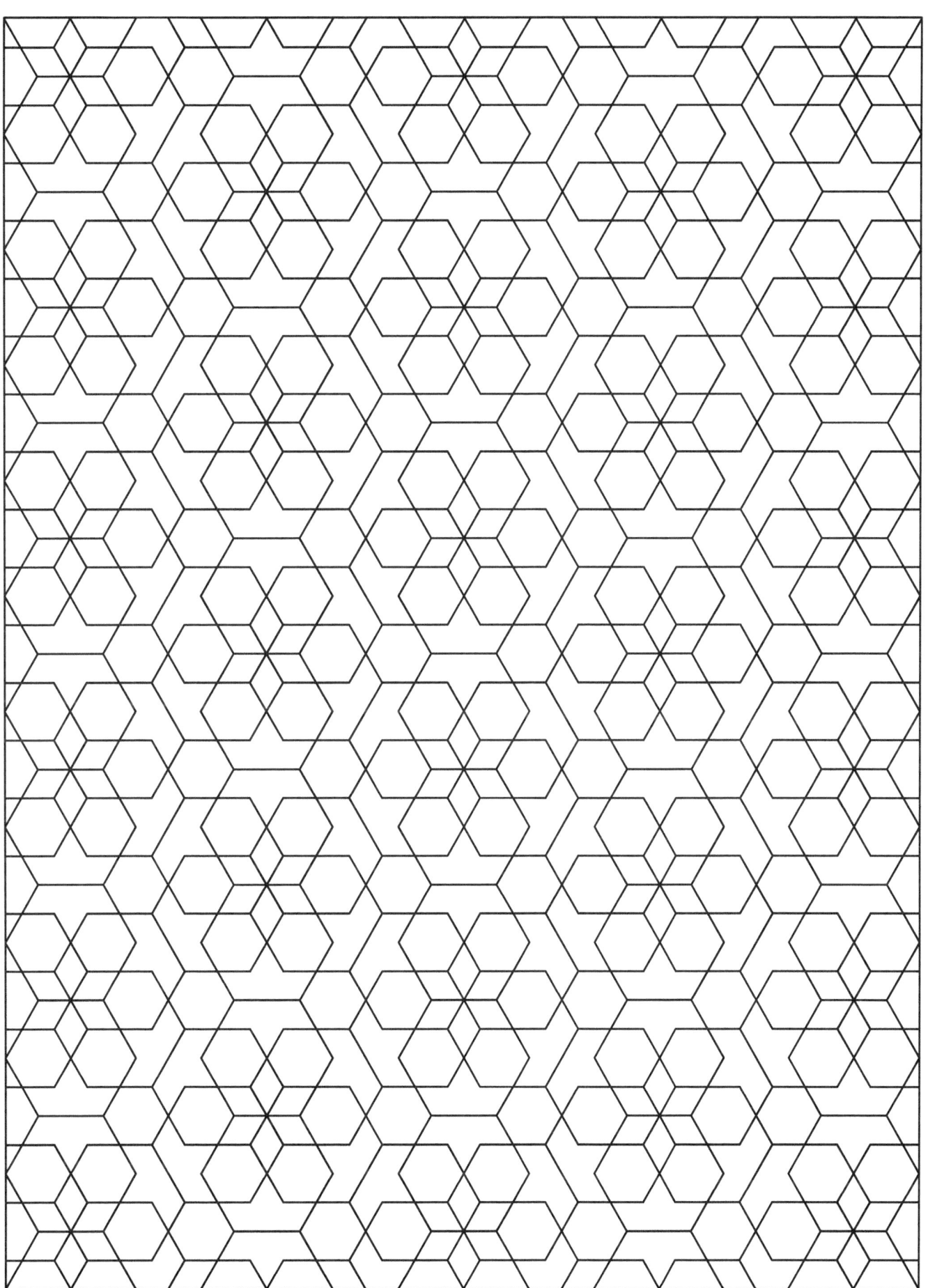

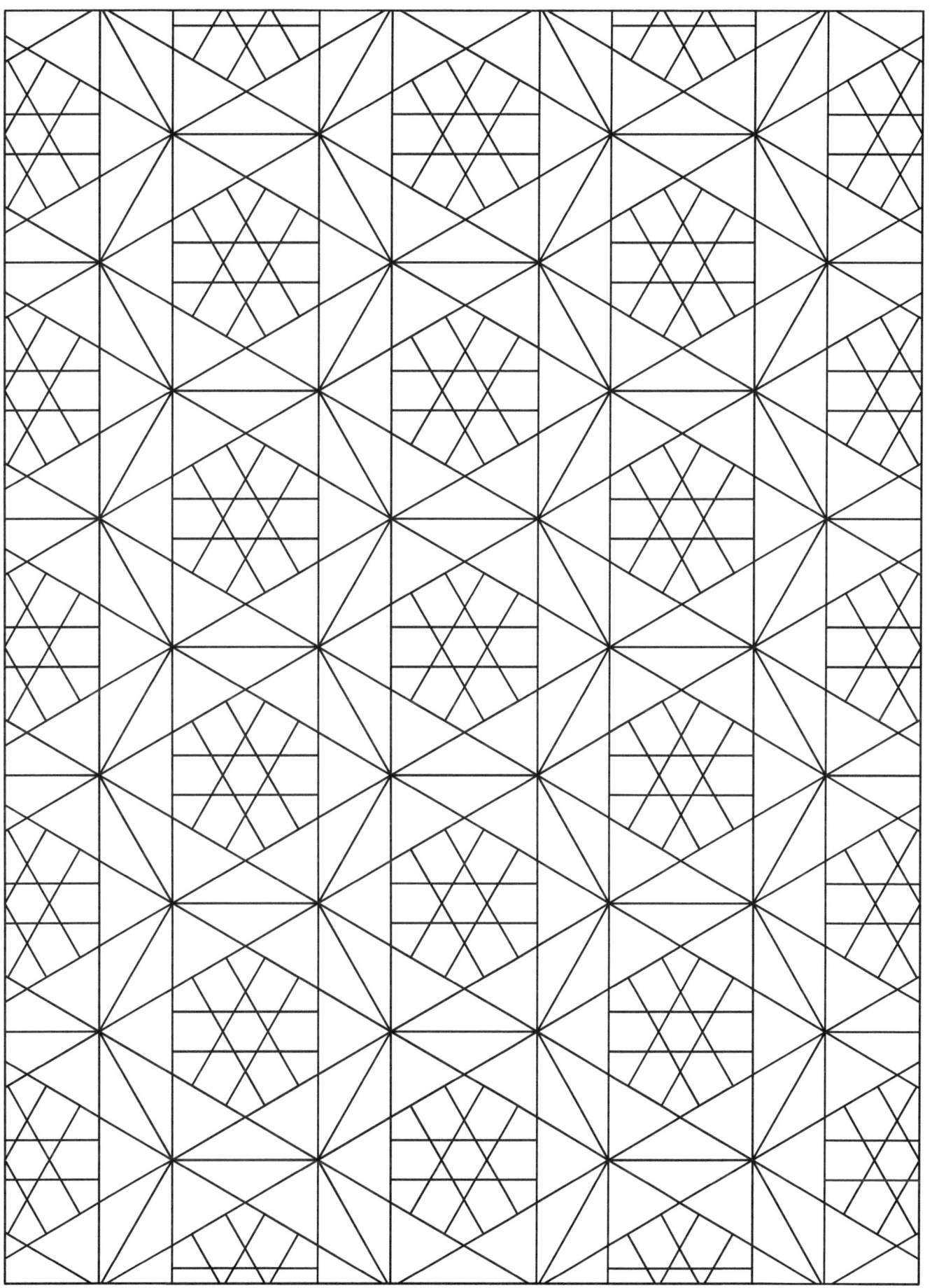

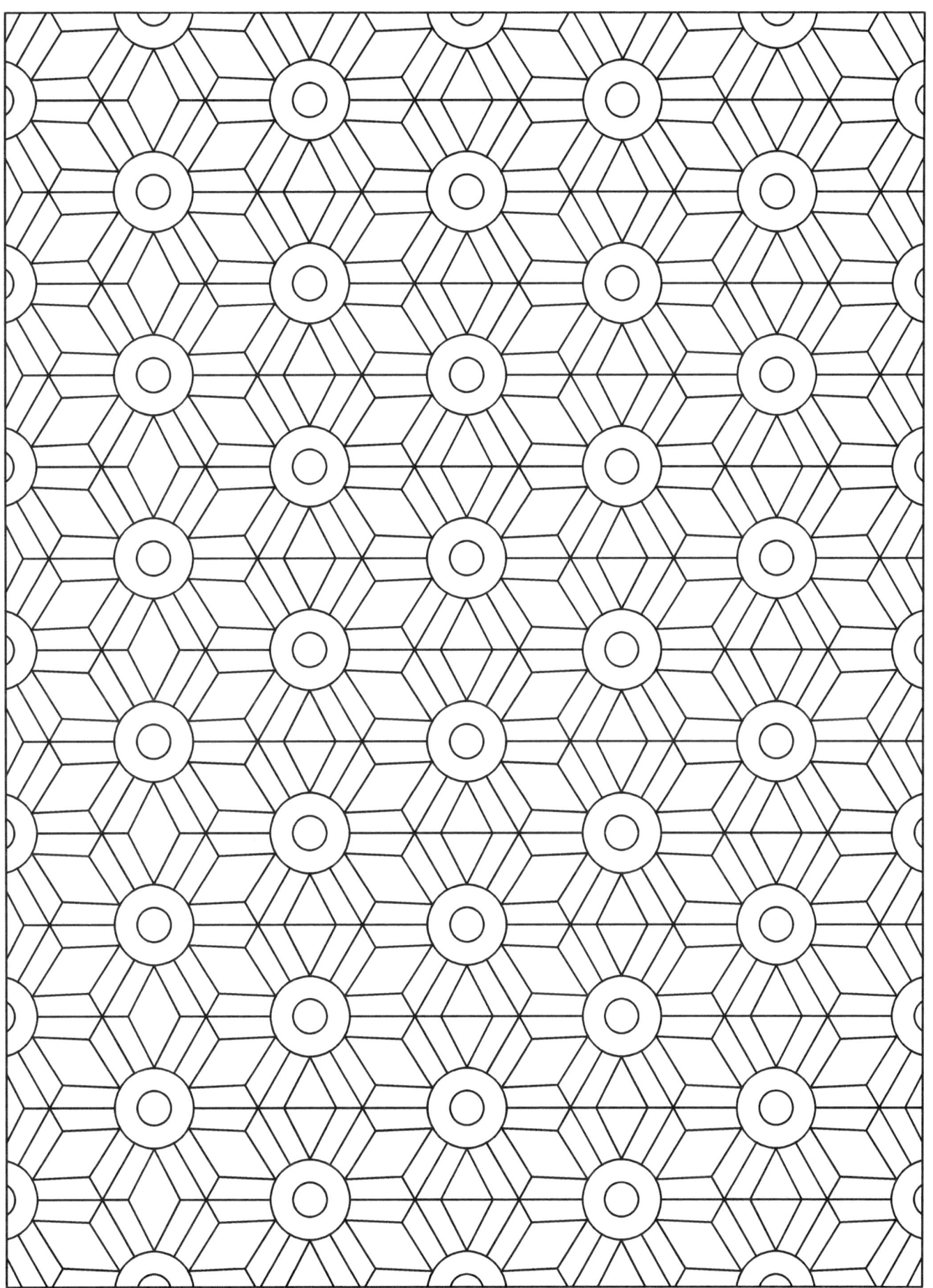

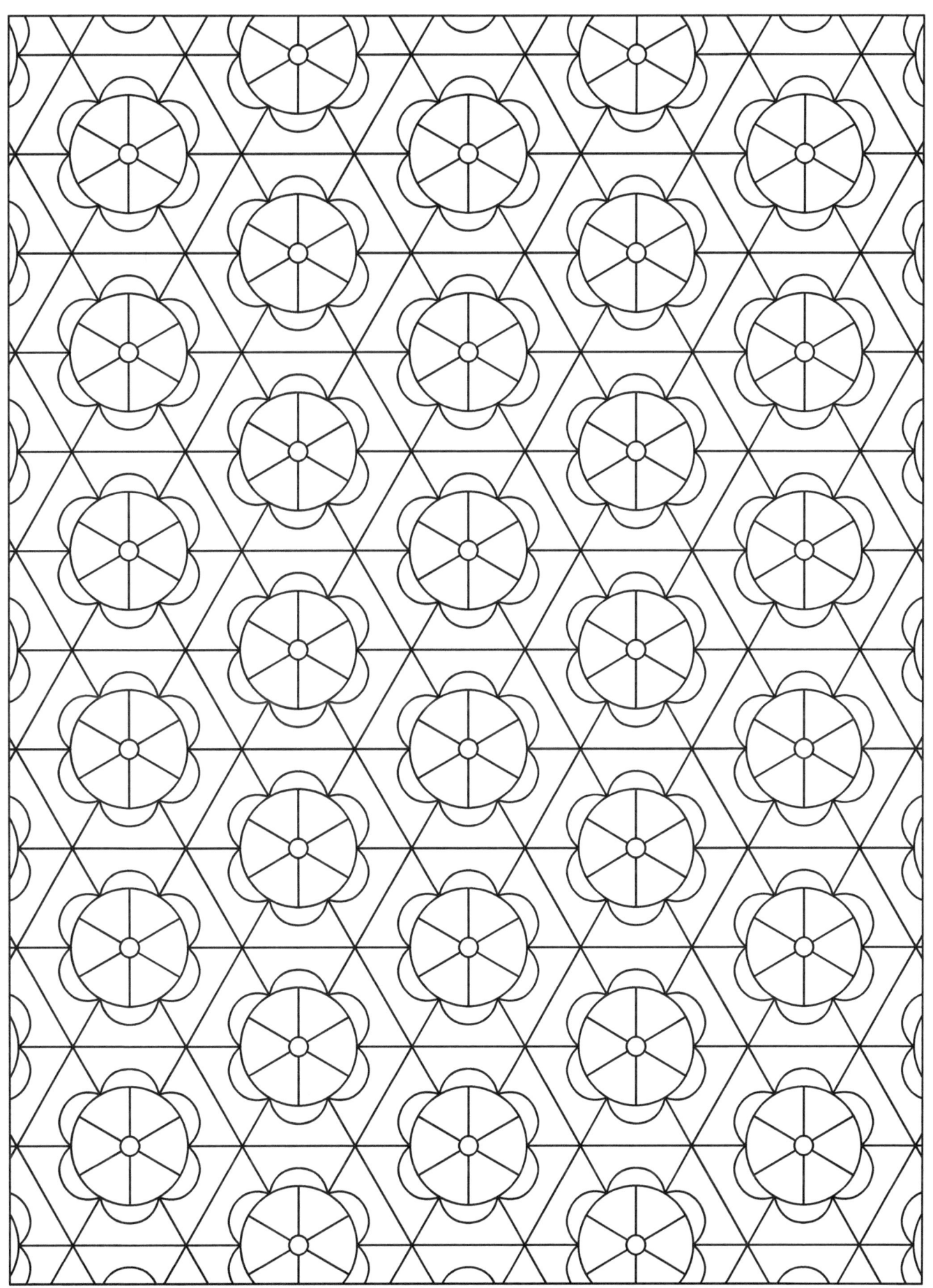

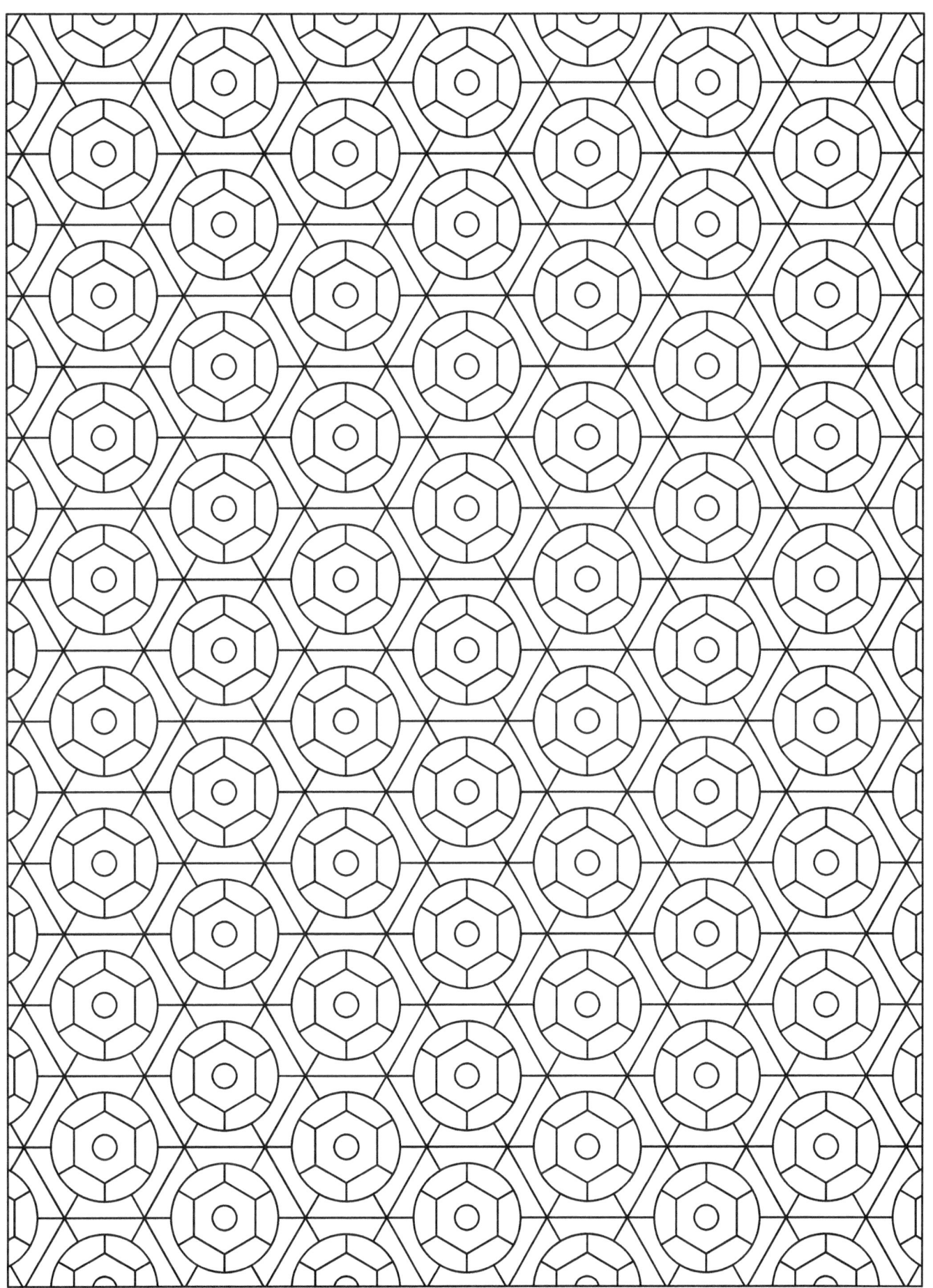

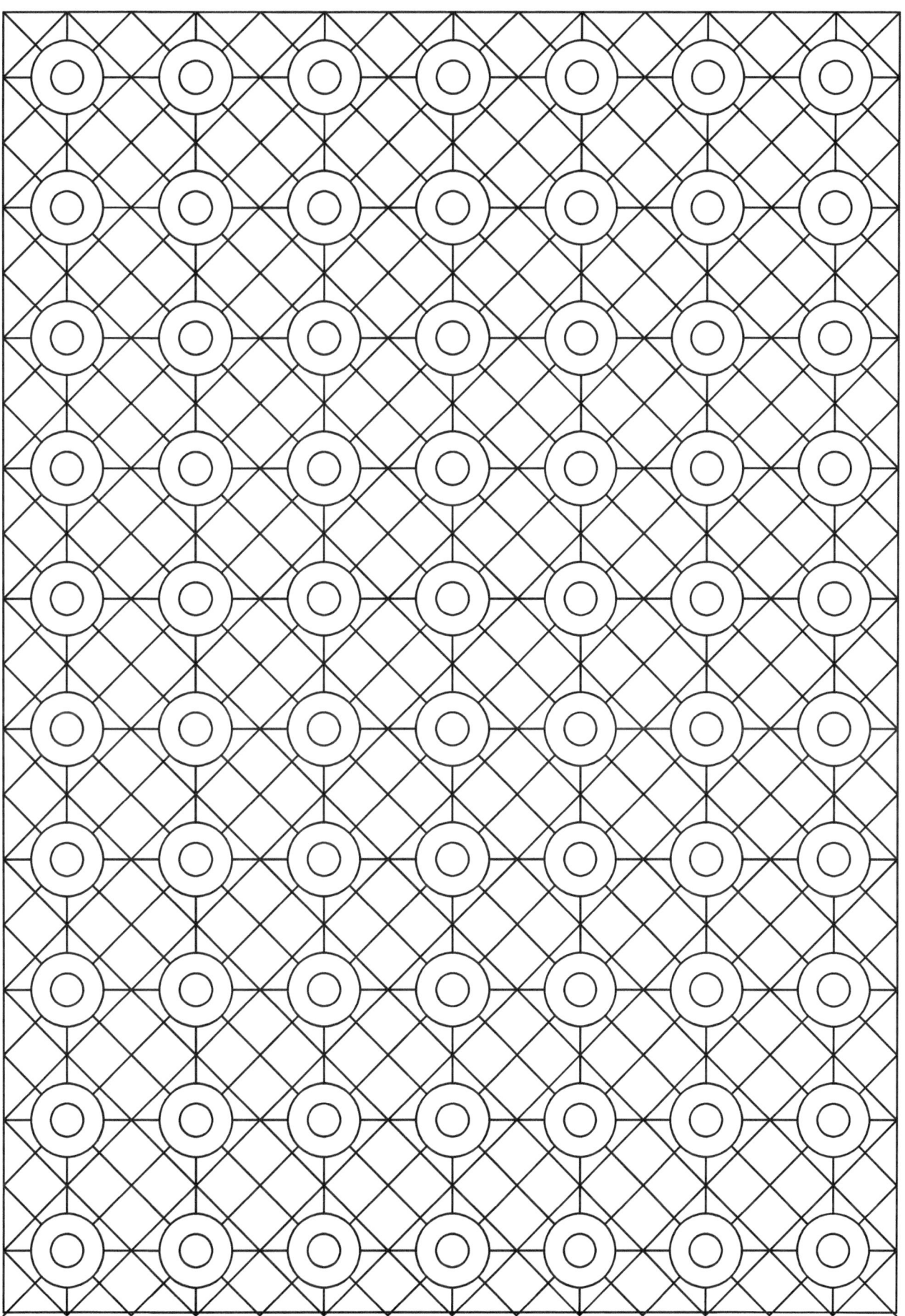

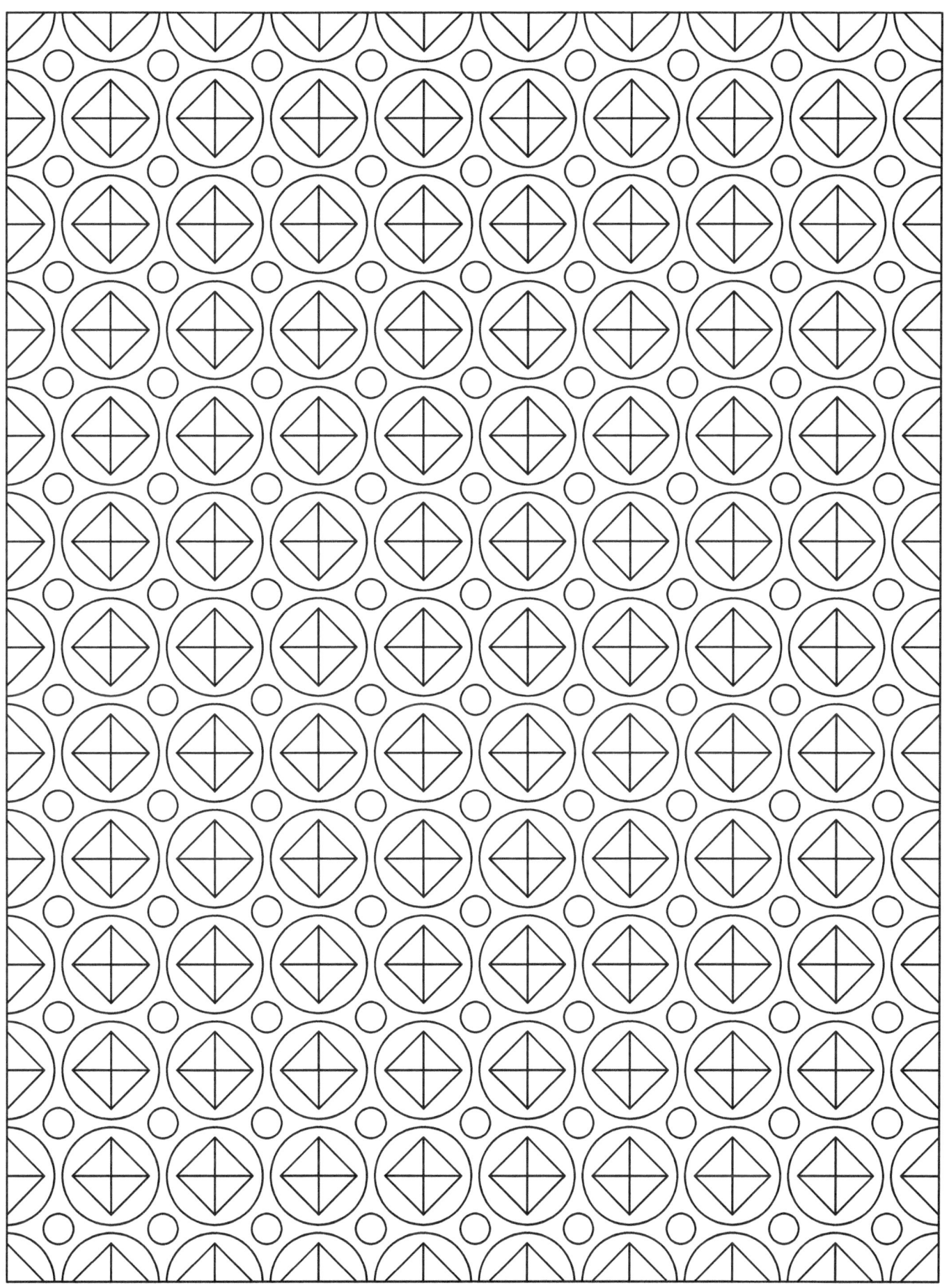

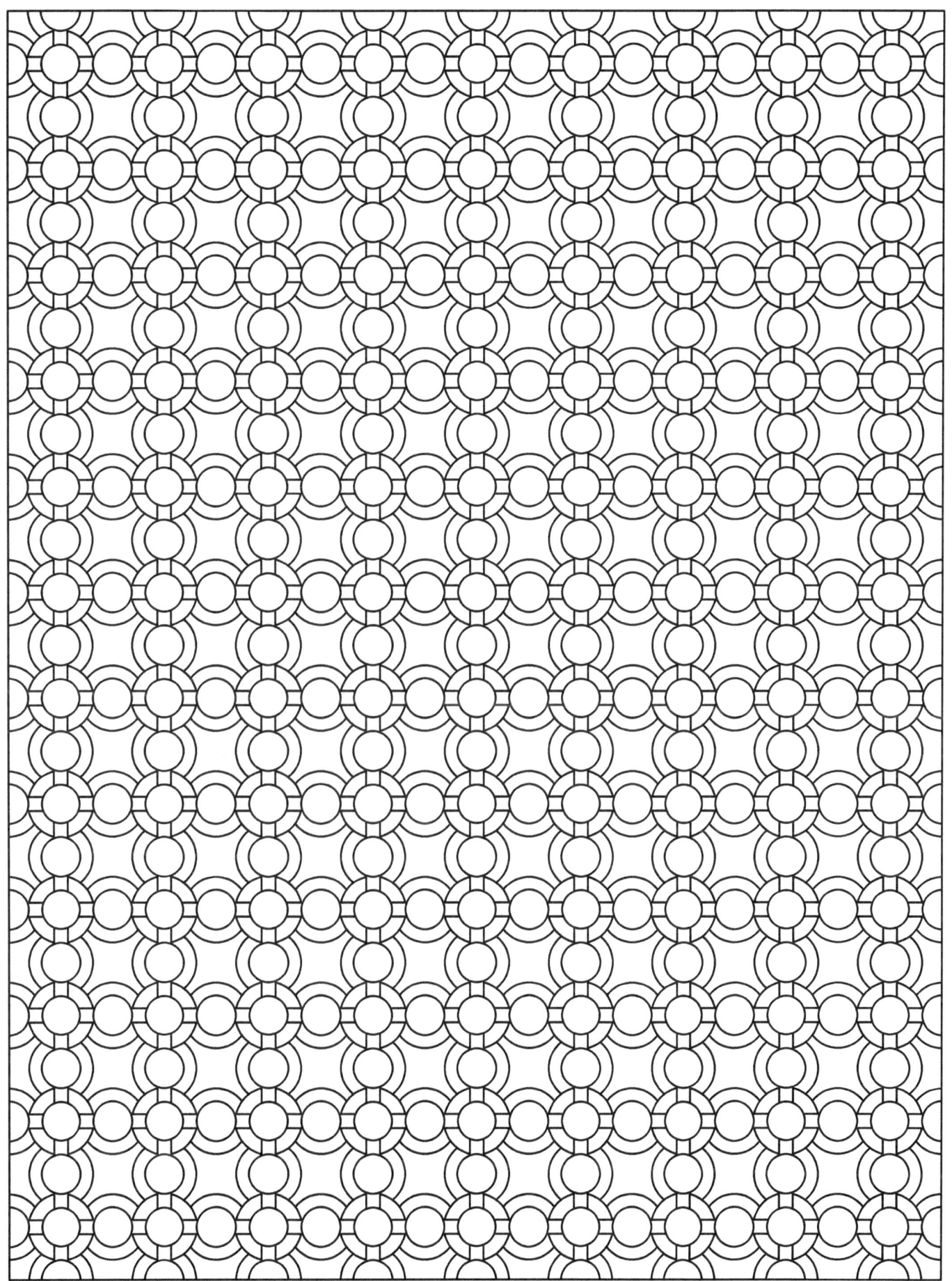

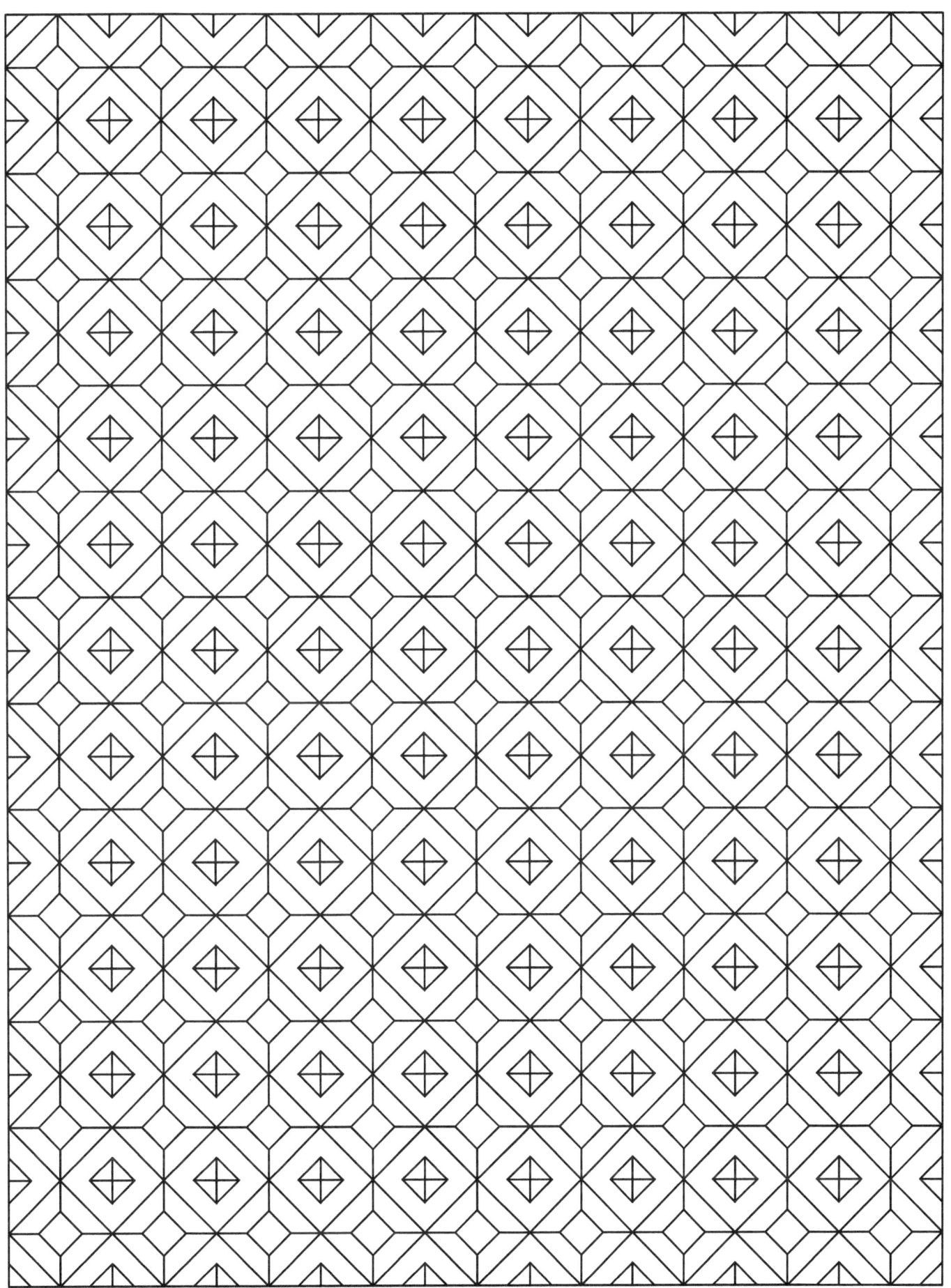

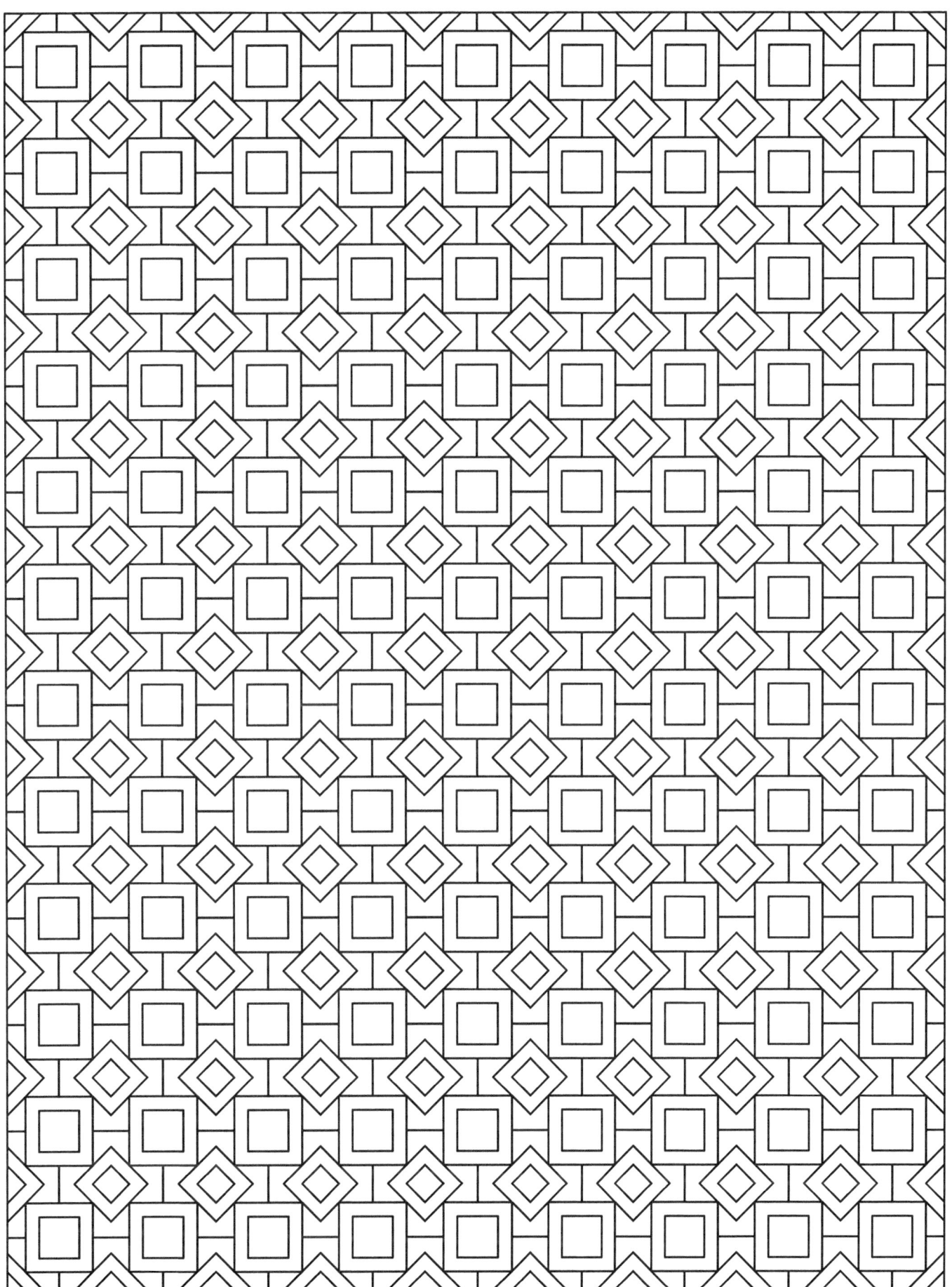

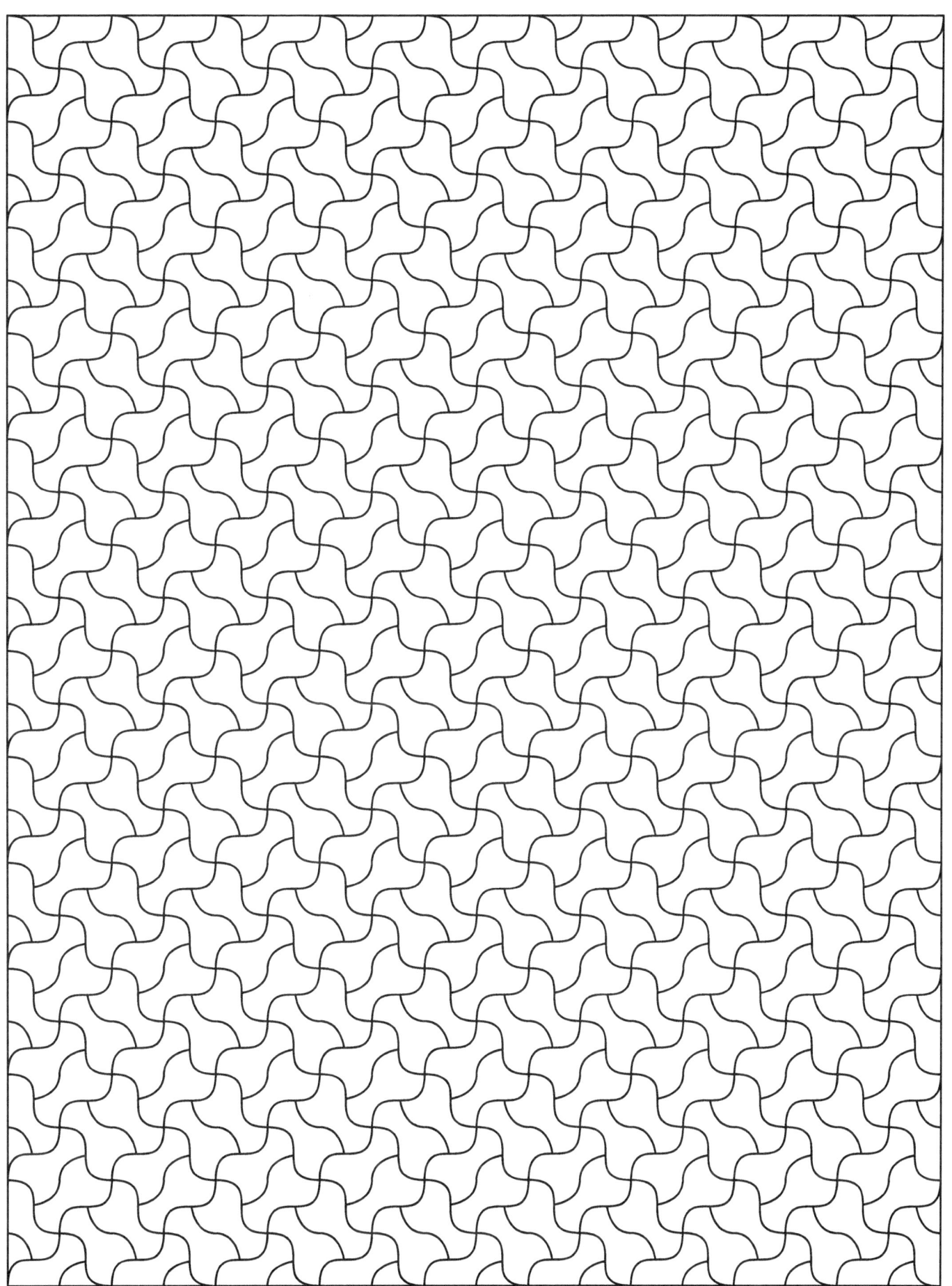

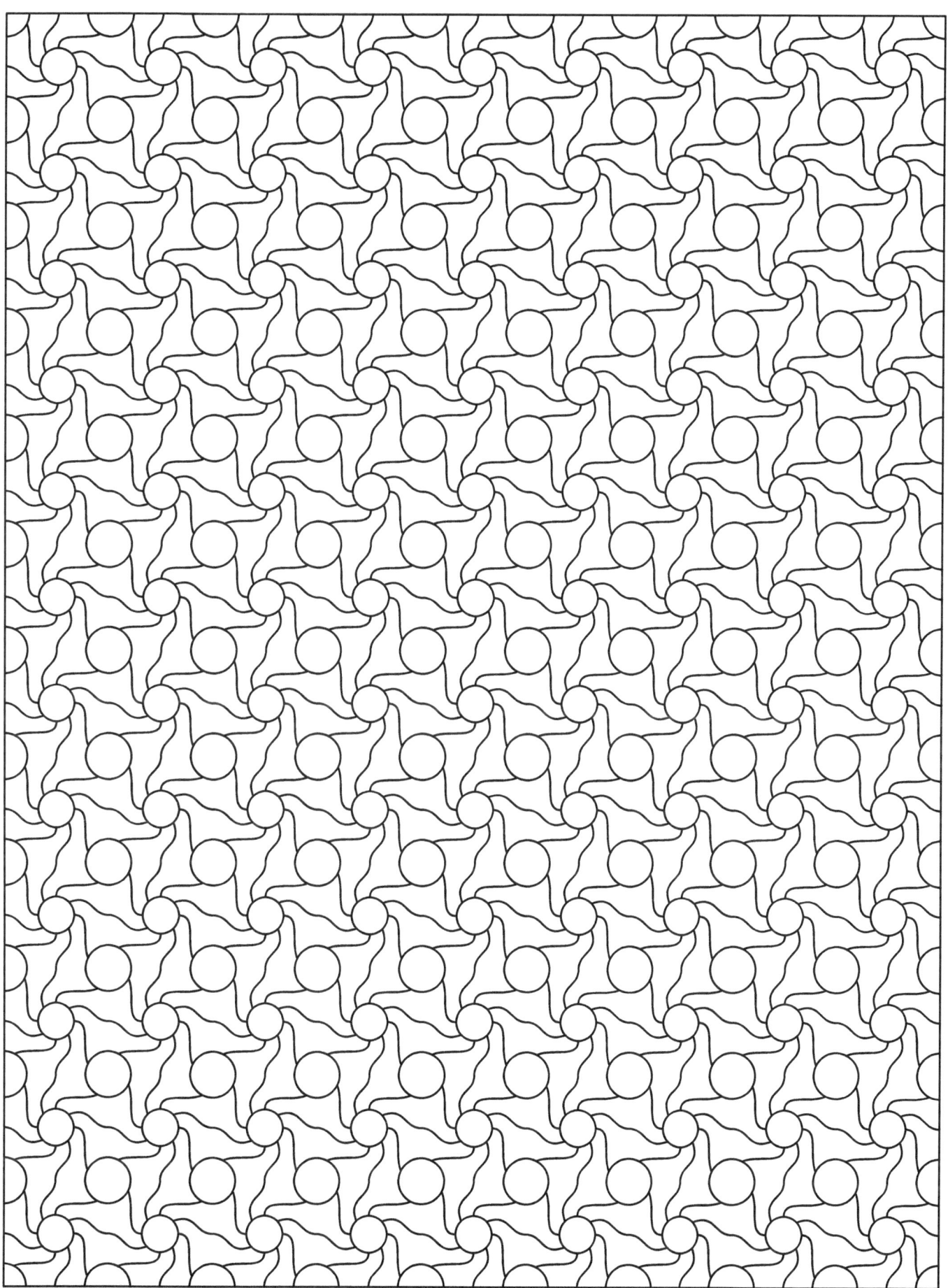

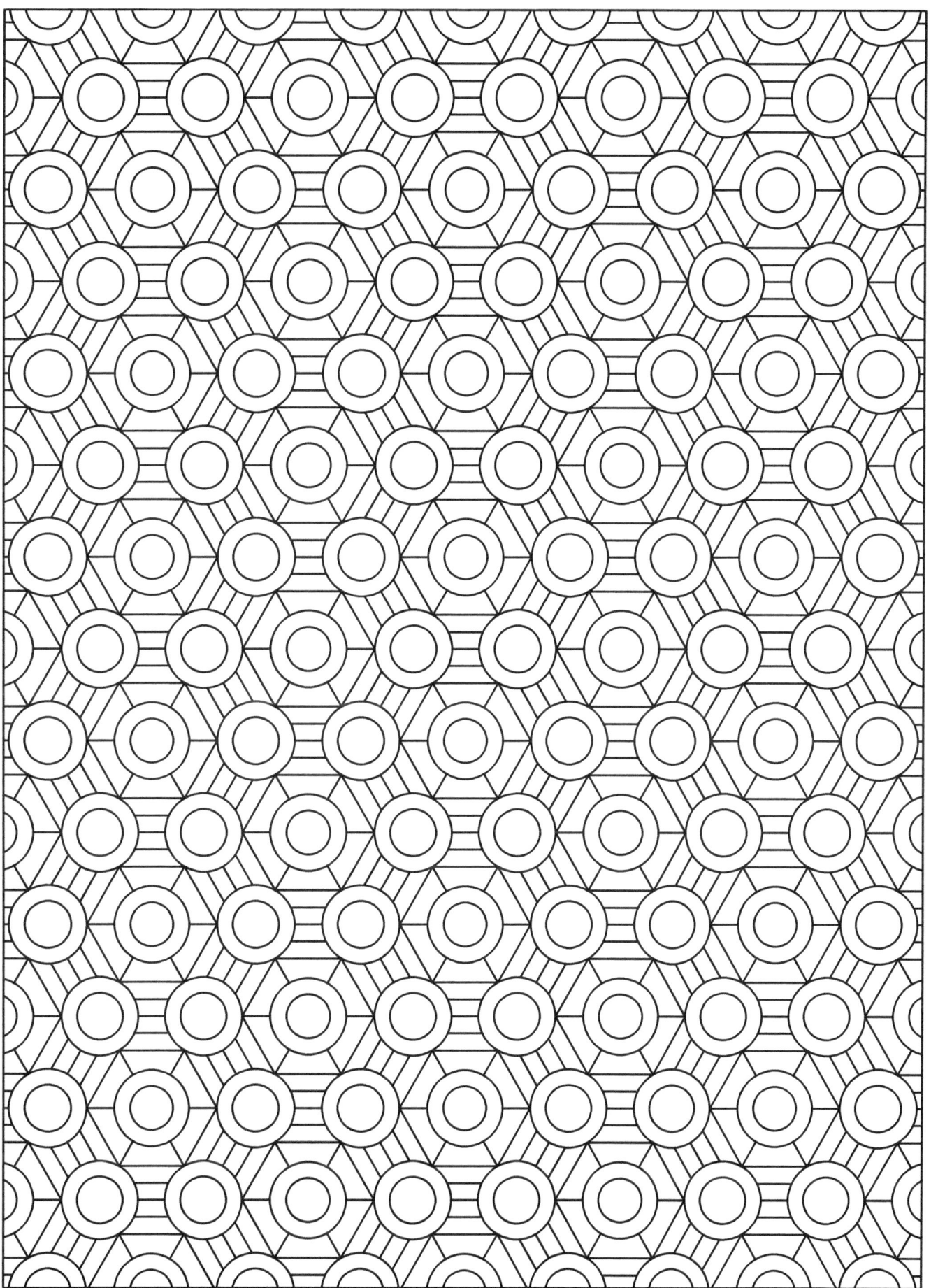

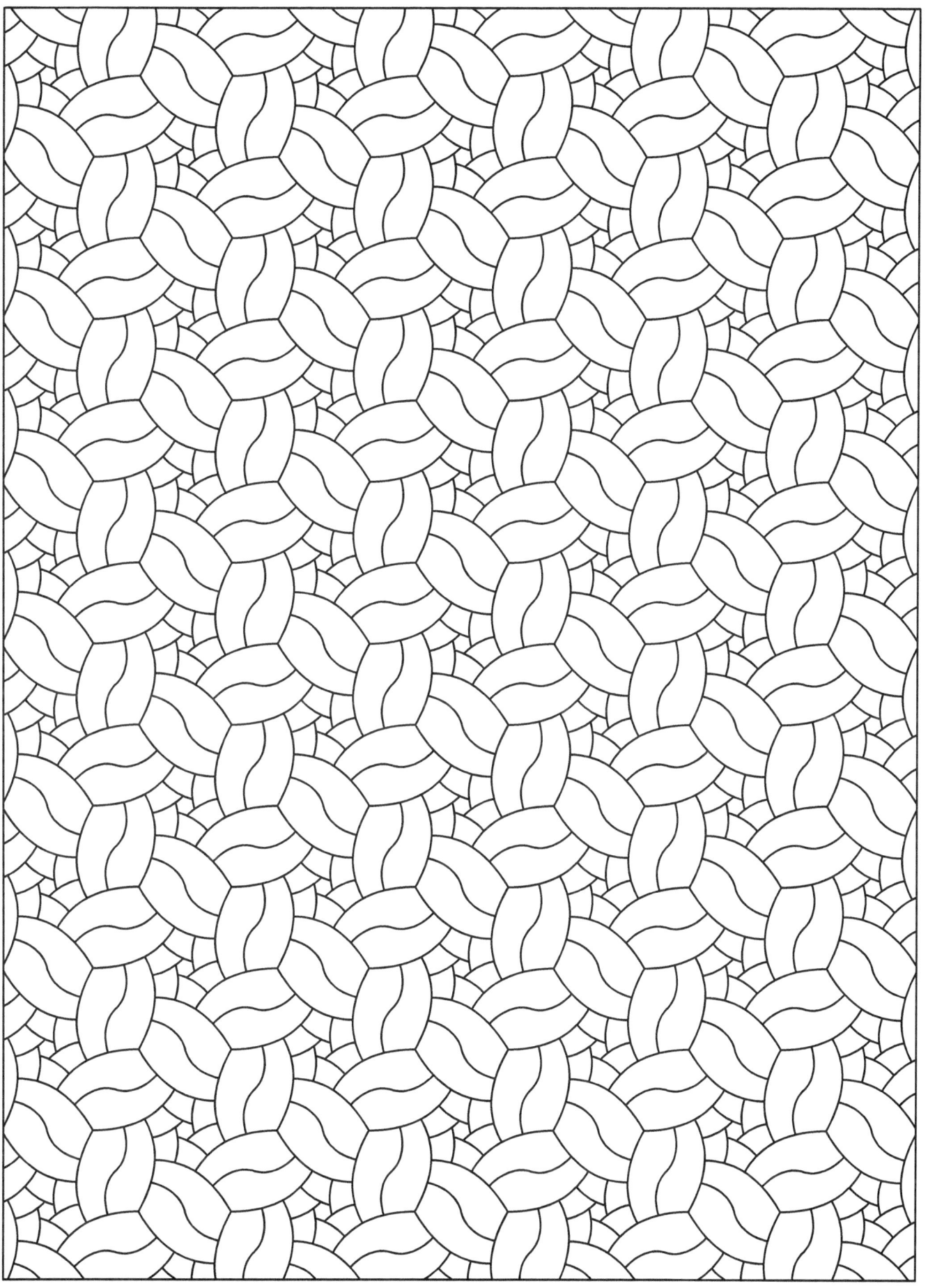

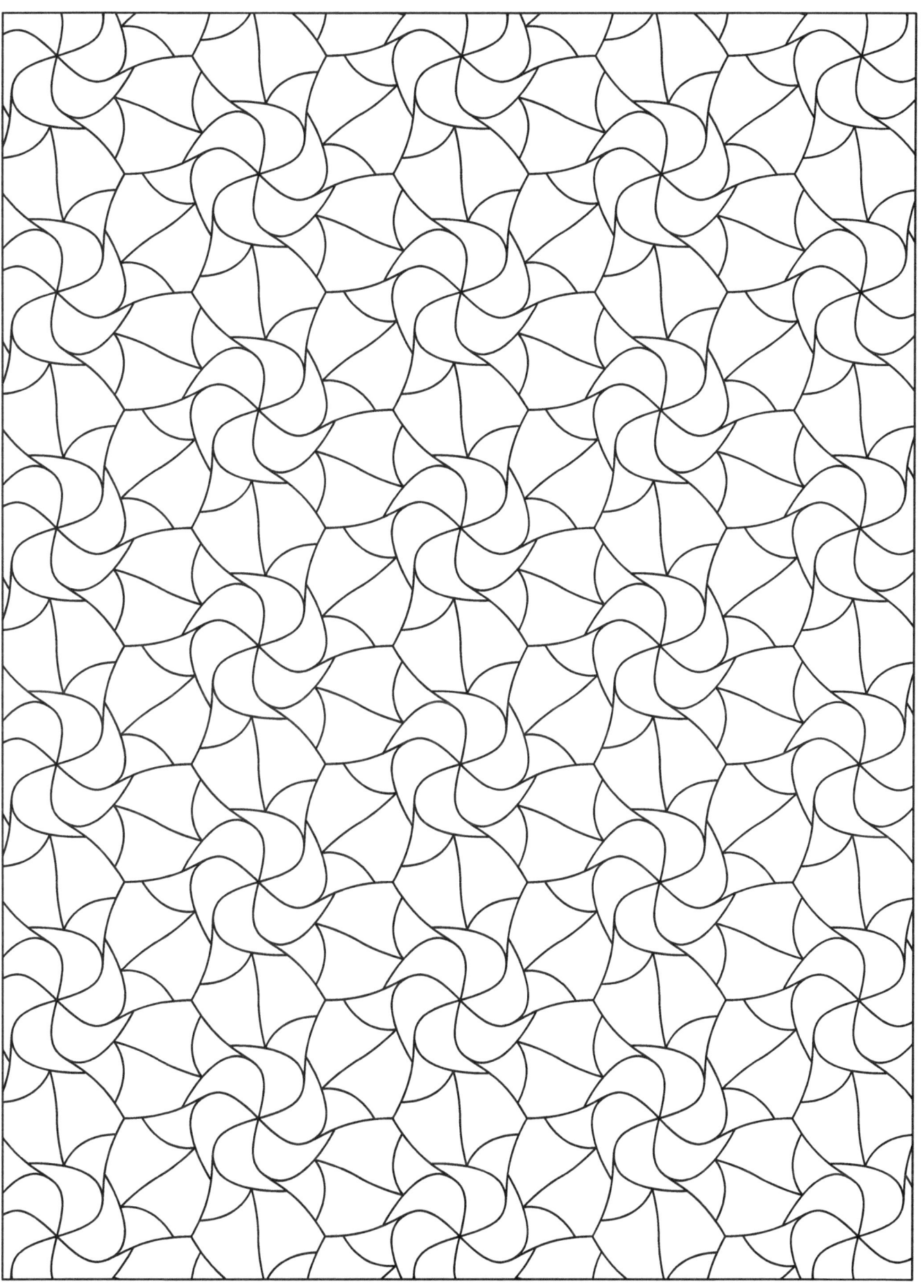

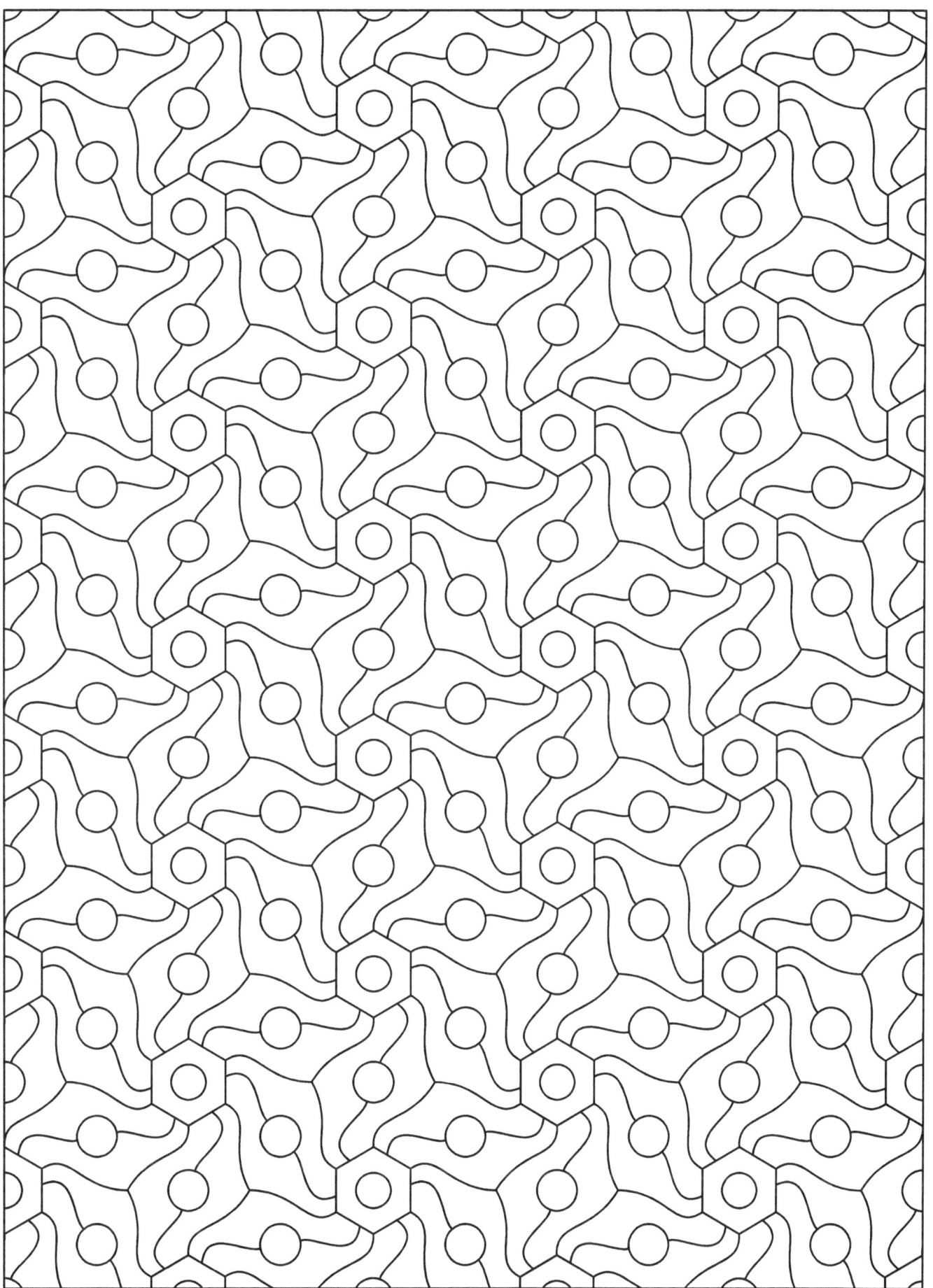

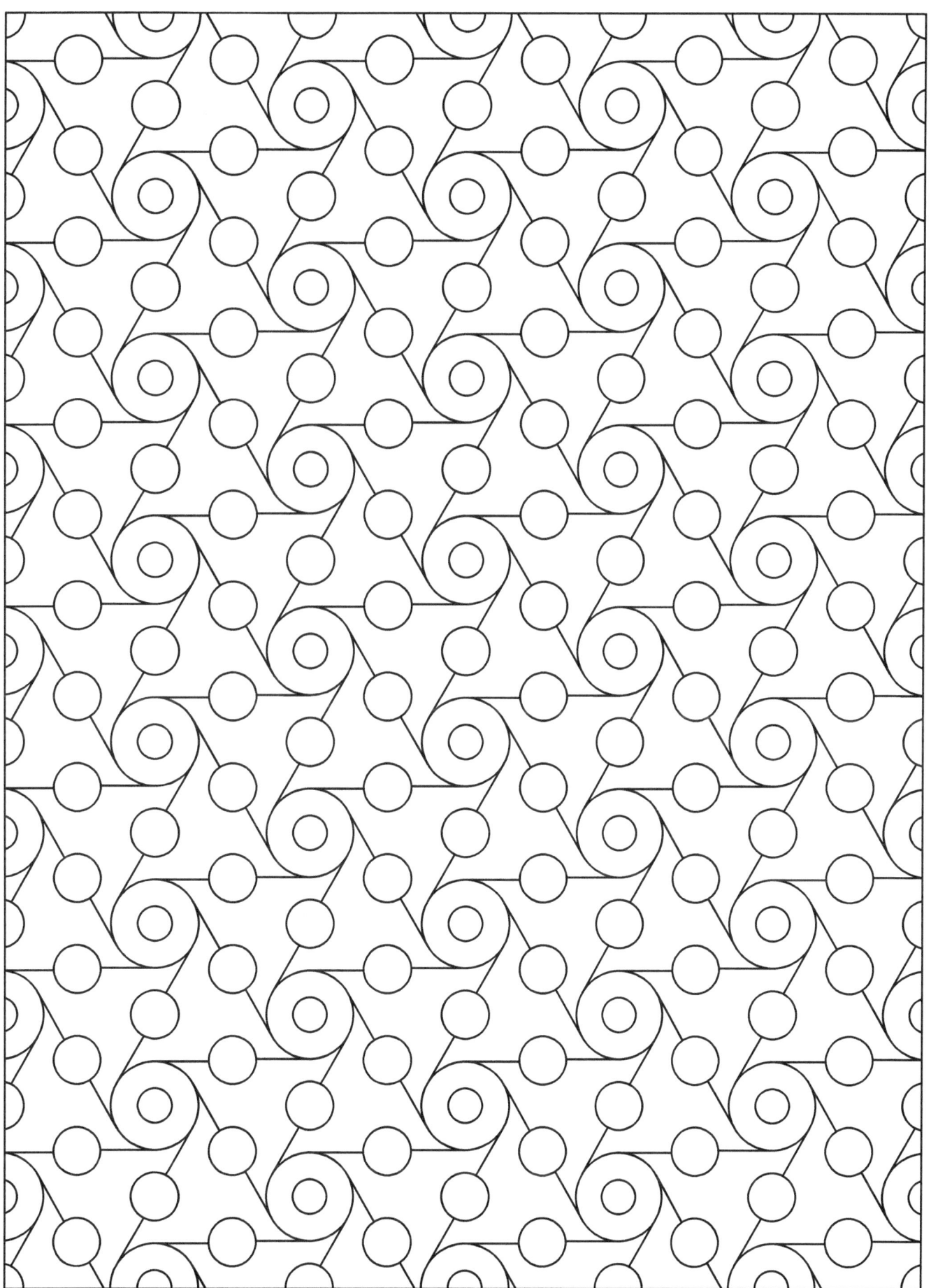

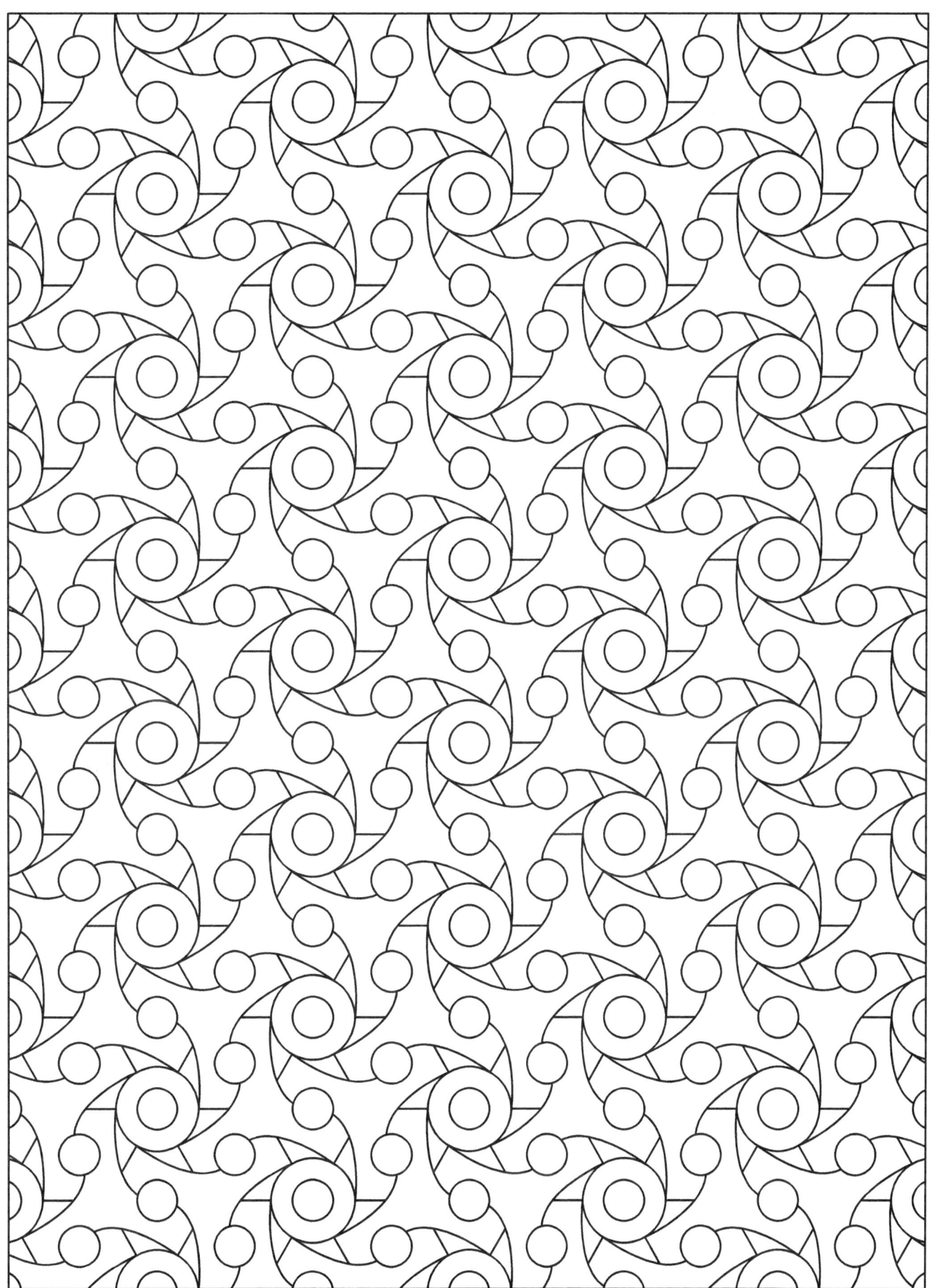

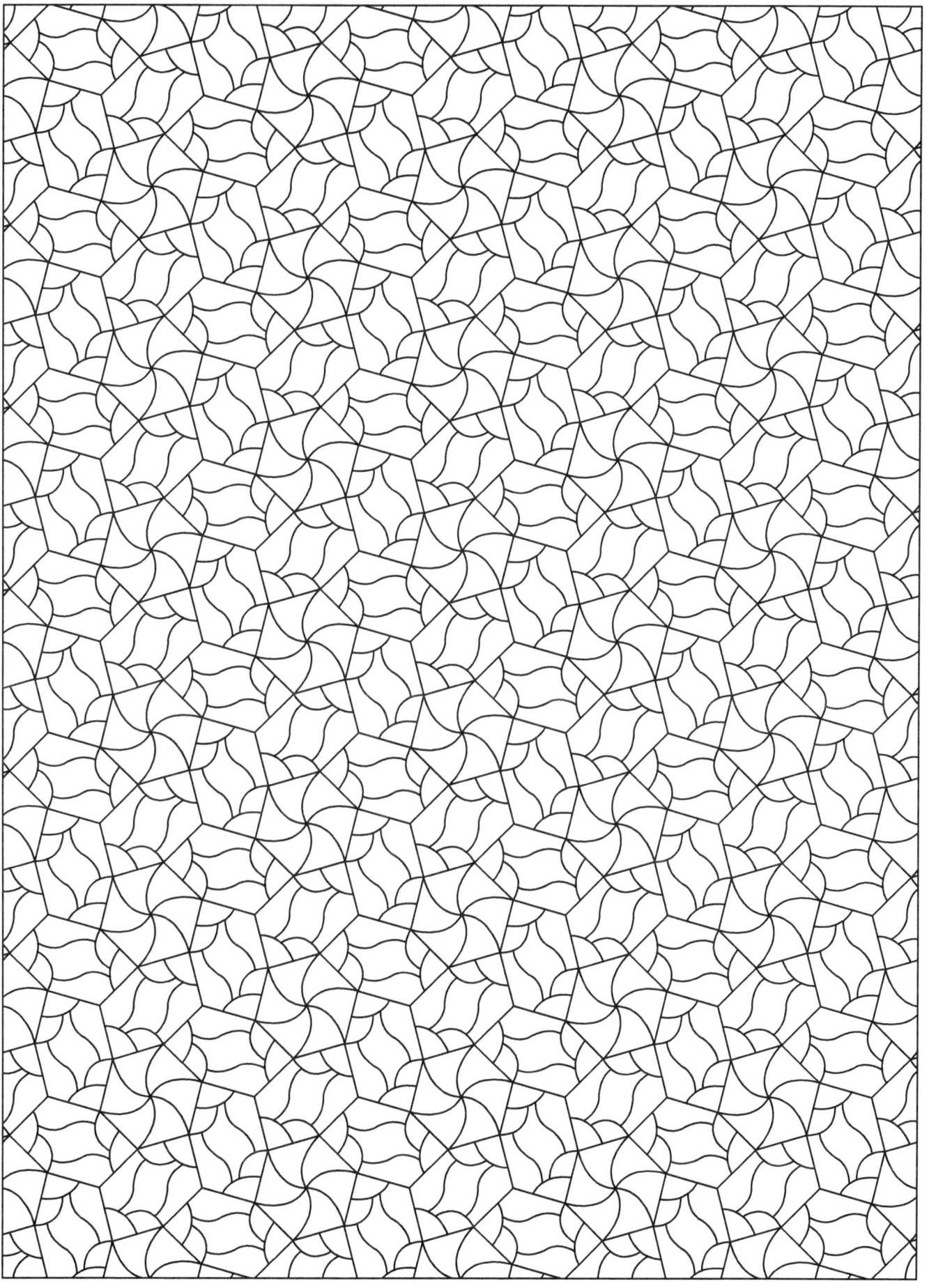

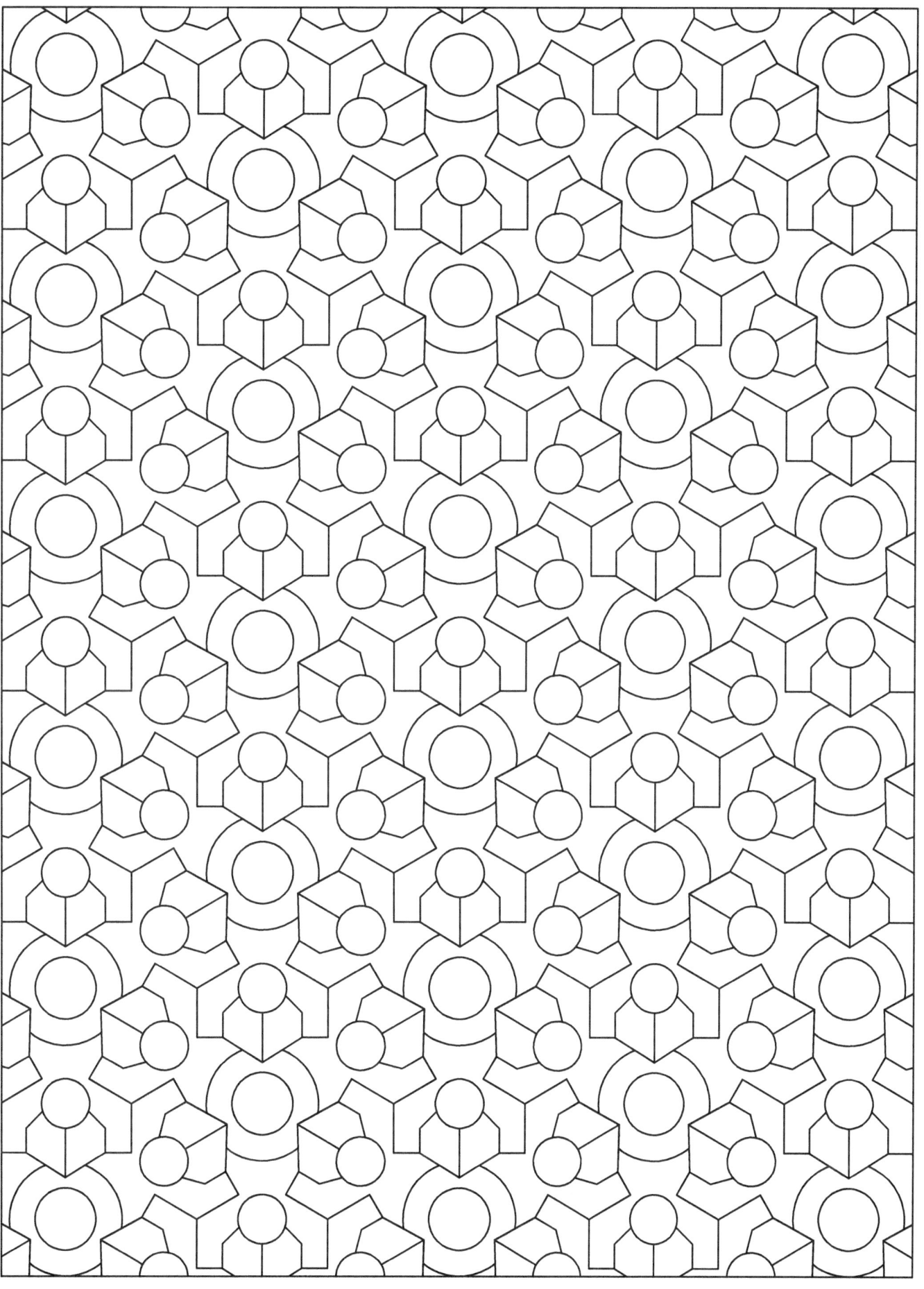

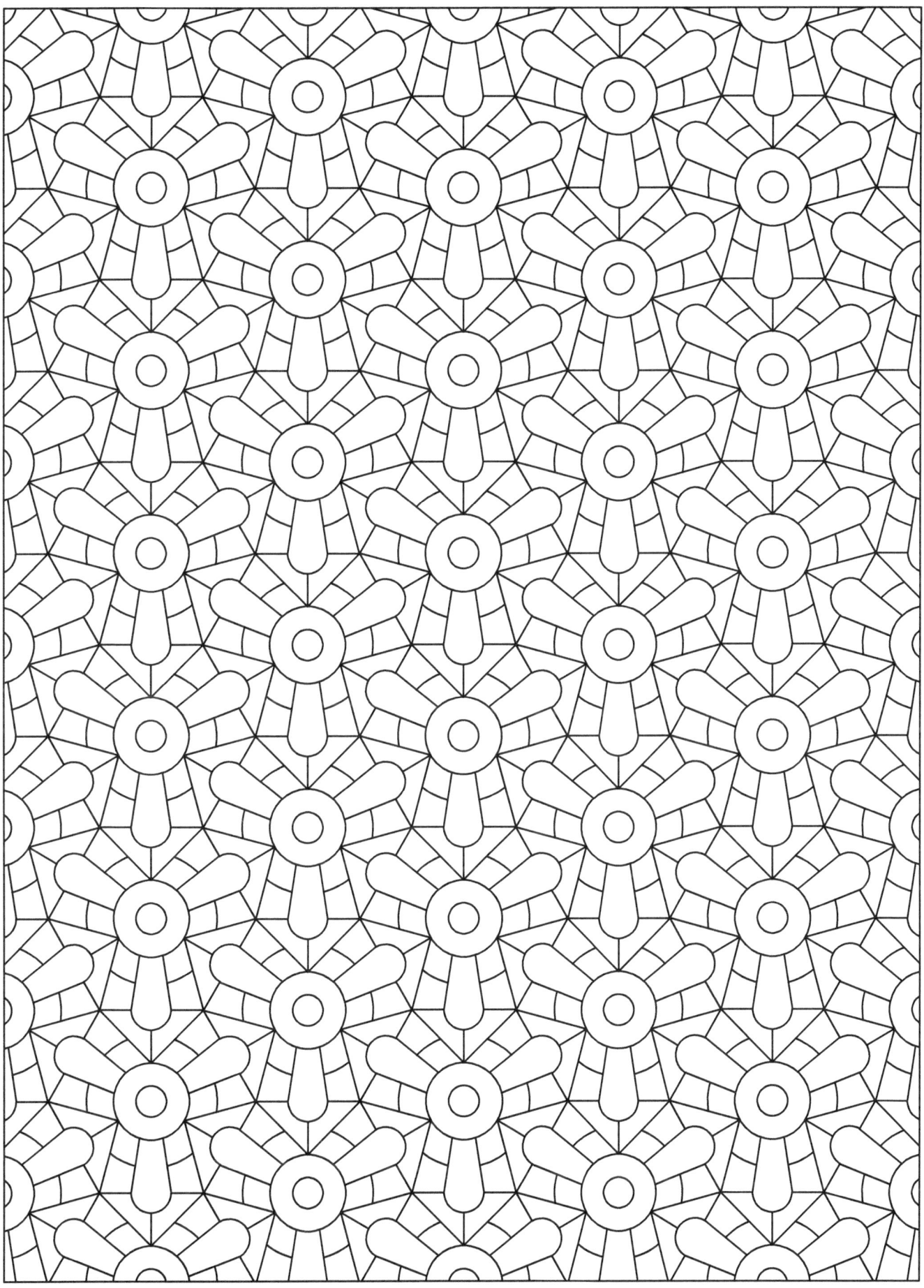

www.ingramcontent.com/pod-product-compliance
Lightning Source LLC
Chambersburg PA
CBHW080451240526
45468CB00026BA/2097